The Crowd in American Literature

Also by Nicolaus Mills

Comparisons: A Short Story Anthology
American and English Fiction in the Nineteenth Century
The Great School Bus Controversy
The New Journalism: An Historical Anthology
Busing USA

The Crowd
in American Literature

NICOLAUS MILLS

Louisiana State University Press

Baton Rouge and London

AAZ2495

PS
169
C75
M54
1986

11/1986
Am. Lit.

Designer: Albert Crochet
Typeface: Linotron Trump Mediaeval
Typesetter: G & S Typesetters, Inc.
Printer: Thomson-Shore, Inc.
Binder: John H. Dekker & Sons, Inc.

Chapters II and III herein appeared previously, in slightly different form, as
"The Crowd in Classic American Fiction" and "Class and Crowd in Ameri-
can Fiction," in the *Centennial Review*, XXVI (Winter, 1982) and XXIV
(Spring, 1980), respectively.

Library of Congress Cataloging-in-Publication Data

Mills, Nicolaus.
  The crowd in American literature.

  Includes bibliographical references and index.
  1. American literature—History and criticism.
2. Crowds in literature.   3. Mobs in literature.
4. Social classes in literature.   5. Labor and
laboring classes in literature.   6. Social history
in literature.   7. Politics in literature.   I. Title.
PS169.C75M54   1986   813'.009'355   86-3014
ISBN 0-8071-1286-0

For my mother and father
and in memory of Joan Kelly

Contents

Acknowledgments

I am extremely grateful to the Rockefeller Foundation for a Humanities Fellowship that allowed me to do most of the work on this book. I owe a special debt to Lee Edwards, Ann Douglas, Hyatt Waggoner, John Seidman, and my editor at LSU Press, Margaret Fisher Dalrymple. I am also fortunate that territory I cross into has already had such pioneers as Irving Howe, George Rudé, and E. P. Thompson. They have all made my work better.

The Crowd in American Literature

Introduction: The Crowd in Literature

In the middle of Robert Coover's novel *The Public Burning*, his narrator, Richard Nixon, encounters what he thinks is a hostile crowd. It is a moment of testing for Nixon, who immediately identifies his fate with that of the country. "If I turned back now, it would not be simply a case of their bluffing out Richard Nixon, but of the United States putting its tail between its legs and running from a gang of Communist thugs," he insists. For Coover's Nixon, however, it is not enough to be brave. Before confronting the crowd—"lawless rabble," in his words—he instructs the reader as to its nature:

> A mob, you see, does not act intelligently. Those who make up a mob do not think independently. They do not think rationally. They are likely to do irrational things, including even turning on their leaders. Individually, people in a mob are cowardly; only collectively, goaded on by a leader, will a mob appear to act courageously. A mob is bloodthirsty. A taste of blood will whet its appetite for more violence and more blood. Nothing must be done which will tend to accentuate those characteristics. A mob has lost its temper collectively. An individual dealing with a mob must never lose his or he will be reduced to its level, and become easy prey for it. . . . Since a mob is stupid, it's important to confront it with unexpected maneuvers: take the offensive, don't panic, do the unexpected, but do nothing rash.

The joke, it turns out, is on Nixon. What he is sure is a hostile mob is actually a pro-Nixon crowd that wants to see the Rosenbergs electrocuted, and the "typical case-hardened Communist operative" who blocks his path is a fan who wants his autograph.[1]

---

1. Robert Coover, *The Public Burning* (New York, 1977), 207–208.

1

Coover's joke is not a silly one. His Richard Nixon may be mistaken in his judgment of this crowd, but the stereotype he offers sums up the way most of us look upon crowds. The crowd is not a phenomenon we regard as a natural part of our political landscape, and like Coover's Nixon, when we come across one, we prepare ourselves for a bad experience. The crowd, we have been told, is an irrational mass, not an institutional alternative or the embodiment of democratic hopes. In our heart of hearts we believe, as John Keegan writes in *The Face of Battle*, that "a crowd is the antithesis of an army, a human assembly animated not by discipline but by mood, by the play of inconstant and potentially infectious emotion."[2]

The consequences of seeing the crowd in such narrow terms have been pointed out in recent years by historians on both sides of the Atlantic; most notably by E. J. Hobsbawm, George Rudé, and E. P. Thompson in Europe and by Jesse Lemisch, Pauline Maier, and Gordon Wood in America.[3] In their studies of popular movements, they have not only increased our awareness of the role of the crowd, they have made us see its complexity. No longer is it possible to equate the crowd with the qualities—fickle, impulsive, violent, and lower class—that have been used to stereotype it ever since Gustave Le Bon, the founding father of crowd psychology, published his *La Psychologie des foules* [*The Crowd*] in 1895.[4] Thanks to the historical perspective George Rudé and others have provided, we

2. John Keegan, *The Face of Battle* (New York, 1977), 173.
3. George Rudé, *The Crowd in History* (New York, 1964), 3–15, 195–258; E. J. Hobsbawm, *Primitive Rebels* (New York, 1959), 1–12; E. P. Thompson, "The Moral Economy of the English Crowd in the Eighteenth Century," *Past and Present*, L (February, 1971), 76–136; Jesse Lemisch, "Jack Tar in the Streets: Merchant Seamen in the Politics of Revolutionary America," *William and Mary Quarterly*, XXV (July, 1968), 371–407; Gordon S. Wood, *The Creation of the American Republic, 1776–1787* (New York, 1972), 319–28; Pauline Maier, *From Resistance to Revolution* (New York, 1972), 3–26; Alfred F. Young (ed.), *The American Revolution: Explorations in the History of American Radicalism* (DeKalb, Ill., 1976), 233–71, 449–62.
4. Le Bon begins *The Crowd* by insisting that the current claims of the masses hark back to a "primitive communism" and include the "elimination of all the upper classes for the benefit of the popular classes." This view is strengthened by his observation that civilizations have been "created and directed by a small intellectual aristocracy, never by crowds." From time to time Le Bon does admit that crowds can show virtue and heroism, but these

are in a position to challenge the kind of observation Freud makes in his *Group Psychology and the Analysis of the Ego*, where he contends that the crowd "wants to be ruled and oppressed," and to see as equally misleading the ahistorical bias that prompts Elias Canetti in *Crowds and Power* to emphasize the destructiveness of the crowd as its "most conspicuous quality." We now know that crowds are in fact capable of great restraint, frequently are guided by traditional rather than revolutionary values, and often draw their strength from the most stable groups in a nation. Above all, we know that the crowd has altered the face of modern society, making possible changes that institutions and rulers would never have consented to if left on their own.[5]

When we turn to literature, however, we find that the crowd has been a neglected phenomenon. The few critics who have taken note of the role the crowd plays in literature have invariably limited their comments to a text or two, and those most sensitive to the relationship between literature and popular movements—such scholars as Irving Howe, Frederic Jameson, and Raymond Williams—have never given the crowd their sustained attention.[6] That this should be the case is not surprising. Since literature is so often concerned with the individual, the subtle, the paradoxical, it is easy to see why the crowd would not present itself as a likely subject for analysis

---

declarations are overshadowed by his attacks on the crowd. Le Bon finds crowds "only powerful for destruction," "intellectually inferior to the isolated individual," "the slave of impulses," "especially guided by unconscious considerations," and prone to "excessive suggestibility" (*The Crowd* [New York, 1962], 16, 18, 19, 18, 33, 36, 59, 39). Rudé in *The Crowd in History*, 9, argues that Le Bon "was inclined to treat the crowd in *a priori* terms: as irrational, fickle, and destructive; as intellectually inferior to its components; as primitive or tending to revert to an animal condition."

5. Sigmund Freud, *Group Psychology and the Analysis of the Ego* (New York, 1959), 10; Elias Canetti, *Crowds and Power* (New York, 1962), 19; Rudé, *The Crowd in History*, 3.

6. Irving Howe, *Politics and the Novel* (Cleveland, 1957); Frederic Jameson, *The Political Unconscious: Narrative as Socially Symbolic Act* (Ithaca, 1981); Raymond Williams, *Culture and Society, 1780–1950* (Garden City, 1960). See the following books for a discussion of specific crowds in literature: Walter Blair, *Mark Twain and Huck Finn* (Berkeley, 1960), 309–21; Walter Benjamin, *Charles Baudelaire: A Lyric Poet in the Era of High Capitalism* (London, 1973), 52–67; Jeffrey Mehlman, *Revolution and Repetition* (Berkeley, 1977), 42–132.

but instead evoke the kind of response Larzer Ziff makes in his essay "Whitman and the Crowd."

> Literature may be about individuals or about communities— about distinguishing moral characteristics or about shared social views—and, of course, it may be about the interplay of the two. But the crowd at best is but a backdrop. To make it expressive is to attribute to it the personality and body of an individual, and given the crowd's defining feature—its sheer magnitude—that personality can only be one of fickle passion and that body can only be one that engages in gross action.

Even more to the point, the most memorable crowds in literature do seem to mirror the updated version of Le Bon's crowd that Richard Sennett described in *The Fall of Public Man* in noting that modern images of the crowd have made us regard it as "the mode in which the most venal passions of men are most spontaneously expressed." We judge the crowd as "man the animal let off his leash," and "the people actively expressing their feelings in crowds are usually seen as the *Lumpenproletariat*, the underclasses, or dangerous social misfits."[7]

When we think of American literature, we tend to picture a crowd on the order of the vicious lynch mob in William Faulkner's *Intruder in the Dust*. Little changes when we turn to European literature. The differences between Elizabethan England and Victorian England do not seem important when it comes to the behavior of the crowd. In Shakespeare's *Julius Caesar* it is a crowd of Caesar's admirers, the "tag-rag people," as Casca derisively calls them, who kill Cinna the poet because he has the same name as Cinna the conspirator. In Charles Dickens' *A Tale of Two Cities* it is the impoverished men and women of Saint Antoine, advancing like a "remorseless sea," who establish the bloody course the French Revolution will take.[8]

This stereotyping is compounded, moreover, when we switch from specific crowds to the idea of a crowd. It is a literary commonplace for the words *crowd*, *mob*, and *riot* to be used as negative symbols or figures of speech. In Gray's "Elegy

7. Larzer Ziff, "Whitman and the Crowd," *Critical Inquiry*, X (June, 1984), 585; Richard Sennett, *The Fall of Public Man* (New York, 1978), 299.
8. *Julius Caesar*, I, ii, and III, iii; Charles Dickens, *A Tale of Two Cities* (New York, 1970), 249.

Written in a Country Church Yard" the "madding crowd" is assumed to be a source of strife. In Tolstoy's *War and Peace,* when Prince Andrew is disgusted with the troops, he thinks, "This is a mob of scoundrels and not an army," and in Conrad's *Heart of Darkness* the dense Congo jungle reminds Marlow of a time "when vegetation rioted on the earth."[9]

What happens when we begin to look closely at the crowd in literature? When we go beyond seeing it in terms of stereotypes and realize that it appears in a rich variety of forms? The most immediate result is that our reading of specific texts changes. It becomes significant that students, not just the poor, appear on the barricades in Victor Hugo's *Les Misérables* and that the enraged miners of Emile Zola's *Germinal* overrun everything in their path but refuse to attack a pit guarded by a seventy-year-old fellow worker. But equally important is the broader social analysis that coming to terms with the crowd in literature makes possible. In the texts in which it plays a key role, the crowd is not just crucial in its own right. It is a critical lens that enables us to see the following differently:

The dimensions of society. Our sense of what constitutes society in literature is immediately changed by our perception of the crowd. Literary critics have traditionally seen society in terms of class and manners—what Lionel Trilling calls a "culture's hum and buzz of implication"—and then gone on to argue that society comes to life in literature as class and manners manifest themselves in family relationships, marriages, social climbing, and competition among different social groups.[10] When we look at the crowd as a component of society, none of these other elements disappears, but what does happen is that society takes on new dimensions. It manifests itself in a rawer, more fluid form than is customary, and in those settings in which traditional social structures have become inadequate, we see the crowd turn into an instrument of collective expression, sometimes even a substitute for institutions. In European literature the classic case of the crowd playing such a role is in Zola's *Germinal,* where the crowd

9. Leo Tolstoy, *War and Peace* (New York, 1966), 177; Joseph Conrad, *Heart of Darkness* (New York, 1963), 34.
10. Lionel Trilling, *The Liberal Imagination* (Garden City, 1953), 200.

expresses the moral and economic vision of the miners of Montsou with a force beyond that of the church or any individual family. In America we find the crowd occupying an equally decisive role under very different circumstances in *The Scarlet Letter*. Indeed, in Nathaniel Hawthorne's novel the crowd not only serves as a vehicle for punishing people with a vindictiveness that goes beyond the letter of the law; at key moments it becomes the embodiment of Puritan religiosity.

Sources of power. Nothing the crowd does changes the fact that when we look for sources of power in literature, we can count on the traditional ones—money, birth, social position—to be crucial. But in settings where society is in flux or breaking down, the crowd adds a political dimension we tend to ignore. In the classic American novel, we see the repressive side of this political dimension in Mark Twain's *Huckleberry Finn*. There the key to preserving slavery turns out to be neither the law nor the most prestigious slaveholders but a "vigilance committee" of armed farmers who are willing to go after any escaped slave and risk their own lives to put down a suspected slave rebellion. Most significantly, however, the crowd in literature represents a vital source of power for those at the bottom of society. It has the potential to convert the one thing the poor can claim as their own, their bodies, into a strength that can counteract the might of those at the top of society. In Henry James's *The Princess Casamassima* his working-class hero, Hyacinth Robinson, fantasizes leading the "myriad miserable out of their slums" and awakening "the gorged indifferent to a terror that would bring them down."[11] The fantasy fails to materialize for Hyacinth, but in working-class novel after working-class novel, the strike and the labor riot are crucial, and those who participate in them, especially when they have the innocence of Zola's Etienne Lantier or John Steinbeck's Tom Joad, are transformed. Afterwards, they can never go back to leading ordinary lives or feel passive about their status as workers.

Who the people are. For the poor, the collective release that comes when they form themselves into a crowd is often the

11. Henry James, *The Princess Casamassima* (New York, 1964), 243.

first step toward self-liberation, but in literature the rise of the crowd can have the further effect of giving the people, whether we mean by that word the populace or society at large, an identity. Too often in literature, when we speak of the people, we mean society without a face or at best one or two representative figures. When the crowd is portrayed with care, the need for this kind of ambiguity and critical shorthand is eliminated. In European literature we see the political difference such a full portrait makes in *Les Misérables*, where the crowds that form on the barricades draw from a variety of classes and types, but even in the more homogenous crowd of *The Scarlet Letter*, the people are not reducible to a composite personality. Their actions may make them seem as one (especially in the eyes of Hester Prynne), but we quickly realize that some are even harsher than their leaders—and one woman would not have Hester punished at all.

The clarity of the inarticulate. It is not just an identity that an important sector of the population acquires when the crowd in literature is looked at closely—it is also the capacity to demonstrate a clarity of judgment. For a number of historians, writing the history of the inarticulate has been a matter of showing how those who did not have a public voice made subtle and meaningful distinctions as a crowd. But in literary criticism, there is no equivalent body of discovery. The critic concerned with those traditionally written off as inarticulate either turns his attention to a spokesman for the poor (Jim Casey in *The Grapes of Wrath*, for example) or, as in the case of a scholar as innovative as H. Bruce Franklin, he combines orthodox and unorthodox sources (in Franklin's case, fiction and convict writing) to find a people's voice.[12] Understanding the crowd in literature changes this situation. It allows us to look at a traditional body of writing and see masses, not just intellectuals, portrayed as self-aware and reflective. In American fiction we find that both the working poor and the poorest of the poor are constantly making insightful judgments about their situation that never get verbalized. In Theodore Dreiser's

12. H. Bruce Franklin, *The Victim as Criminal and Artist: Literature from the American Prison* (New York, 1978).

Sister Carrie, the striking streetcar workers have the political wisdom to know that only by guerrilla tactics, not all-out confrontation, do they have a chance of winning. And in Ralph Ellison's *Invisible Man,* his Harlemites have enough presence of mind in the middle of a riot to parody white sexual fears and southern lynch law by hanging seven blonde mannequins from a lamppost.

When the crowd in literature is seen in these terms, what emerges is not a new genre we can call crowd literature but rather a new way of thinking about certain texts and the ideas in them. My aim is to show what happens when such a critical approach is tried. But what follows is not a survey, let alone a taxonomy, of the crowd in literature. It is not the crowd in literature in general that I propose to analyze, but a subject more suited to a single essay: the crowd in American literature from the time of the American Revolution to the Great Depression of the 1930s. For this purpose I deal in chronological order with three major crowds: the revolutionary crowd of John Adams and Thomas Jefferson, the majority crowd of the classic American novel, and the working-class crowd of America's social realists. In the last chapter I discuss the rise of the modern media crowd in terms of Ellison's *Invisible Man.*

An inquiry of this sort is of necessity illustrative, detailed, and as a consequence selective. In the chapters that follow I have deliberately centered my analysis on a core of well-known authors and their work. I have given only marginal attention to crowds that from my perspective are sui generis, and I have bypassed such books as William Faulkner's *Light in August* and Walter Van Tilburg Clark's *The Ox-Bow Incident* because to discuss the crowds in them would be to repeat myself. In addition, I have been careful about the types of crowds I describe. It is the political actions of the crowd, not the crowd in general or the crowding of mass society, that concern me, so I have excluded from this study casual crowds—audiences at a theater and gatherings at a fair—as well as crowds that are basically metaphoric in nature. The strolling Londoners of Edgar Allan Poe's "The Man of the Crowd" are not relevant to my argument any more than the throngs of Walt

Whitman's *Leaves of Grass* or the aggregates that in his *Demo-cratic Vistas* symbolize America en masse. Like George Rudé in *The Crowd in History*, I focus on the face-to-face, direct-contact crowds we associate with revolutions, strikes, pro-tests, lynchings, and elections.[13]

At the same time, there are certain critical boundaries it has been essential for me to stretch. Since my subject is the way the crowd has been portrayed in American literature, I have felt free to discuss nonfictional as well as fictional writing. In both genres we can see how our writers' perceptions of the crowd, even the language they use to describe it, have evolved over the years. This is especially true of the eighteenth cen-tury—the writings of Adams and Jefferson provide the best analysis we have of the revolutionary crowd and more than live up to Garry Wills's observation in *Explaining America* that our nation's "first entirely developed art was political literature."[14]

I have also tried to be as free as possible from restrictive judgments in the terms I use to describe crowds. The words *crowd, mob,* and *riot* come loaded with pejorative implica-tions, and I thought it important to divest myself of these im-plications wherever I could. When I refer to a crowd, I have in mind no more than a gathering defined by its collective iden-tity or purpose. It may in exceptional cases be a relatively small gathering (the English Riot Act of 1715, for example, de-fined a crowd as twelve or more persons), but as a rule, when I describe a crowd I mean a gathering that cannot fit into a room but can, on the other hand, be contained in a public hall or square. I use the word *mob* as sociologists now do, to desig-nate any active or mobile crowd. Within the context of this study, *mob* is not automatically a synonym for lower-class crowd. As for a riot, I look upon it as what happens when a crowd goes beyond the bounds of demonstration and acts in a violent fashion. I do not assume that the violence of a riot—there is a long history of rioters attacking property rather than

13. My description of the approach I take borrows from Richard Poirier, *A World Elsewhere: The Place of Style in American Literature* (New York, 1966), viii; Rudé, *The Crowd in History,* 3.

14. Garry Wills, *Explaining America: The Federalist* (New York, 1981), xi.

people—is going to be brutal or irrational any more than I assume a mob is going to be brutal or irrational.[15]

By virtue of approaching the crowd in American literature as I do, I cross into territory that a number of historians have staked out in their studies of popular movements. That is as it should be. The crowds I discuss are soaked in history, and understanding the America in which they were conceived helps explain their conduct and composition, and why at various points they have been credited with this or that virtue. But in pursuing this connection, I am not arguing, even covertly, that the crowds of American history and American literature can be looked on interchangeably. What concerns me is what our writers have *thought* the crowd stood for and why this vision—both when it reflects and departs from reality—has been so significant.

To explain this phenomenon, my starting point is the writings of Adams and Jefferson. From the 1770s on, both men found it imperative to describe the crowd, and their diaries and letters, as well as their public papers, reflect their struggle to come to terms with the revolutionary mobs that were playing such an important role in the colonies. Each realized that in a politically divided America, it was not enough to equate the crowd and the patriot cause. It was essential to answer the charge that the crowd menaced the entire social fabric of America, and they sought to do this by putting the role of the crowd in perspective. What emerges from their writings is not, however, what we might reasonably expect: a closely argued but fundamentally self-serving portrait of the revolutionary crowd. Even in their diaries and letters Adams and Jefferson are too complex for that. Their writings instead emphasize the conviction—arrived at slowly and in piecemeal

15. Under the provisions of the Riot Act, twelve or more persons "unlawfully, riotously, and tumultuously assembled together to the destruction of the public peace" could be required to disperse within an hour of the reading of the act. For a discussion of the origins of the term *mob*, see Max Beloff, *Public Order and Popular Disturbances* (London, 1938), 9. On the mob as an active or mobile crowd, see Roger W. Brown, "Mass Phenomena," in Gardner Lindzey (ed.), *Handbook of Social Psychology* (2 vols.; Cambridge, Mass., 1954), II, 840–41. On the relationship between riots and crowd violence, see John Bohstedt, *Riots and Community Politics in England and Wales, 1790–1810* (Cambridge, Mass., 1983), 7.

fashion—that for a crowd to be a legitimate revolutionary force, it must be disciplined and have clear aims, represent the nation as a whole, arise as a last resort, and stem from a political situation in which nothing short of crowd action will do. Adams used these criteria to condemn the patriot mob responsible for the Boston Massacre and to praise the Boston Tea Party, but in the long run they were criteria that served him and Jefferson more like a pair of glasses than a political yardstick, for these standards allowed them to see that the conduct and style of a crowd are as crucial to the way it is perceived as its sheer power. When we turn to such modern studies of the American Revolution as Jesse Lemisch's "Jack Tar in the Streets," Pauline Maier's *From Resistance to Revolution*, and Gordon Wood's *The Creation of the American Republic*, we find that time and again they confirm Adams' and Jefferson's belief that at its best the revolutionary crowd was a representative body and that its targets were, as Maier argues, "characteristically related to grievances."[16]

To what lengths judgment of the crowd can be carried becomes apparent in the next section of this study, which focuses on the classic American novel of the nineteenth century. There, the style and conduct of the crowd are explicit issues. In *The Scarlet Letter* it is a grim "crowd of Puritans" who turn Hester's punishment into a social drama. In *Moby Dick* it is the crew of the *Pequod*, "welded into oneness," who pursue the White Whale with a moblike fury, and in *Huckleberry Finn* it is a "crowd" of fifteen armed farmers who go after Jim when he escapes.[17] What has changed between centuries is the political direction of the crowd. No longer is it an anticolonial or liberating force. It is closer to the kind of crowd Leonard L. Richards analyzes in *"Gentlemen of Property and Standing,"* where he observes that the anti-abolition mobs of the Jacksonian era "were neither revolutionary nor lower class. They involved a well-organized nucleus of respectable, middle-class citizens who wished to preserve the

16. Wood, *The Creation of the American Republic*, 319–20; Maier, *From Resistance to Rebellion*, 13.
17. Nathaniel Hawthorne, *The Scarlet Letter* (Columbus, 1963), 56; Herman Melville, *Moby Dick* (Indianapolis, 1964), 701; Mark Twain, *Adventures of Huckleberry Finn*, ed. Walter Blair and Victor Fischer (Berkeley, 1985), 336.

status quo rather than to change it. . . . Frequently they had either the support or the acquiescence of the dominant forces in the community."[18] Tocqueville's fear of the "tyranny of the majority" captures the feelings Hawthorne, Melville, and Twain have about the crowds they describe. In their fiction the crowd is dangerous not because it is the vanguard of a rampant democracy but because of its loyalty to authority and willingness to pursue antidemocratic ends. Over and over, the crowd devotes itself to leveling whatever or whomever is exceptional and at the height of its anger vents its wrath on a target—an adulterous woman, an albino whale, a runaway slave—that is symbol and scapegoat for a multitude of dissatisfactions. The result in the classic American novel is a vision of the crowd far darker than that of Adams or Jefferson and one that goes beyond worry over unleashed masses. In the midst of an era of nationalism and expansion, it reflects an abiding fear that in America democratic men are the enemy of democratic man.

The opposite is the case with the working-class crowd we find in William Dean Howells' *A Hazard of New Fortunes,* Dreiser's *Sister Carrie,* and Steinbeck's *In Dubious Battle* and *The Grapes of Wrath.* Poor and victimized by those in authority, this crowd desperately wants more: more money, more power, more recognition of its needs. What it challenges on those occasions when it rises up are not individual freedoms but the social and economic structure of the country. The political conditions that this crowd faces are ones in which, as labor historian Jeremy Brecher observes, social order depends on the "threat—and employment—of private, police, and military armed force."[19] It is, however, sadness and not anger that in the end characterizes the working-class crowd described by Howells, Dreiser and Steinbeck. The source of their crowd's misery is invariably a corporation or combination of businessmen with enormous financial clout, and when it acts, their crowd rarely faces an accountable personal adversary. Its target is usually property or, when the target has a human face, the police or scab laborers. As a result,

18. Leonard L. Richards, *"Gentlemen of Property and Standing": Anti-Abolition Mobs in Jacksonian America* (New York, 1970), 129–30.
19. Jeremy Brecher, *Strike!* (Boston, 1984), 317.

the view we get of the working-class crowd from their fiction is filled with contradictions and paradoxes. Despite the sympathy it elicits, their crowd rarely triumphs, and despite its rage and destructiveness, it ends up the victim of far worse violence than it commits.

The burden of these next chapters is to substantiate this picture (a triptych really), but in the pages that follow I am not interested in simply fleshing out a critical history that argues that the crowd has been a vital force in American literature, sometimes advancing the cause of democracy, sometimes undermining it. Although the American writer's preoccupation with crowds does not signal a uniform ideology on his part, it does signal an interest in masses and collective activity that is anything but neutral in the level of political concern it represents. My aim is to come to terms with this political concern. I want to show what happens when the crowds of American literature with their multiple associations challenge the hegemony of the pastoral and timeless images traditionally used to define the meaning of America.

In its iconography the change I am describing is the equivalent of turning to American art and finding that Gilbert Stuart's portraits of George Washington (with their homage to unblemished nobility) or Asher Durand's *Kindred Spirits* (with its vision of Thomas Cole and William Cullen Bryant surrounded by nature) have less to tell us about a vital part of our past than does Paul Revere's revolutionary engraving *Boston Massacre* (with its patriot mob scene) or George Caleb Bingham's election series (with its motley crowds of voters). But the issues posed by the crowd are not limited to iconography or matters of style. They involve the place and definition of democracy in American literature, most specifically, the political sensibility of American fiction.

Emerson in a notebook passage speaks with uncharacteristic warmth of men acting together, illustrating the relationship of the crowd to the first of these key issues. "All the men in the world cannot make a statue walk and speak, cannot make a drop of blood or a blade of grass any more than one man can," Emerson writes. "But . . . let there be truth and virtue in one man, in two men, in ten men, then there can be concert; for then is concert for the first time possible; now nothing is gained by adding zeroes, but when there is love and truth, these do naturally and necessarily cohabit and concert, cooperate and bless." Emerson is not, of course, talking about crowds here. He saw the crowd as the mob, an "emblem of unreason, mere muscular and nervous motion."[20] He is talking about perfect men doing what perfect man would. And that is just the point. In a country where geography has throughout most of American history given us the option of avoiding closeness and crowding, our most cherished image of democracy is epitomized by man alone in nature or in a symbolic community of two. The analyses of our literature and culture that have followed in the wake of this powerful image reflect this ideal. It is no coincidence that so many of the best modern studies of American writing—Henry Nash Smith's *Virgin Land*, R. W. B. Lewis' *The American Adam*, Leo Marx's *The Machine in the Garden*—stress the timeless and pastoral quality of American life and thought.

The problem is that this critical emphasis now exerts such influence over our reading of American literature that it blinds us to what our writers' portraits of the crowd embody: a vision of democracy in which the way people define themselves collectively is as important as the way they see and perfect themselves individually. At the most obvious level, I am talking about changes in our perception of the scenery of American literary democracy: the inclusion of what is forbidden by Emersonian dictates—masses of the Left and Right, organized violence, urban warfare. But the key issue here goes beyond the ability of the crowd in American literature to provide a dose of reality or a measure of social description that we would otherwise miss out on. Of larger significance is the fact that ignoring the crowd in American literature has meant ignoring our writers' willingness to take seriously a political world in which the extra-institutional alternative is not a retreat into nature or a liberal angst but a banding together, the abandonment of home and isolation for the street and the public square.

20. William H. Gilman *et al.* (eds.), *The Journals and Miscellaneous Notebooks of Ralph Waldo Emerson* (16 vols.; Cambridge, Mass., 1963–1982), VII, 437–38, V, 100.

Like the perfect democracy of Huck's and Jim's raft, the imperfect, sometimes brutal democracy of the crowd tends to be short-lived. Although spurred on by the failure of institutions (or impatience with them), the crowd still represents a political process that must inevitably give way to ordinary social life. Even the calmest of crowds, the Puritans of *The Scarlet Letter* who gather to witness Hester's punishment, soon tire of the pressures on them to be actors in a political drama. But the brief life-span of the crowd, the fact that it provides a holiday from conventional society, does not diminish its importance or reduce it to a side issue for American literature.[21] Rather, it creates a context in which our writers' political concerns may be juxtaposed without fear of false emphasis against their democratic idealism.

The significance of this context for the way we judge American fiction is particularly important. Since the end of World War II, no view of our novels has been more influential than Lionel Trilling's in *The Liberal Imagination* and Richard Chase's in *The American Novel and its Tradition*. With great care and persuasiveness, Trilling and Chase argue that American fiction, in contrast to English fiction, is romance and that as a result of this romantic bent, our novelists resist looking closely at society, contenting themselves instead with heroes whose actions are explicable primarily by the myths and symbolic purities of their character. Society, as Trilling puts it, is "tangential" for our writers, especially the classic American authors of the nineteenth century. Their best work depends on a commitment to abstraction that leaves social actuality behind.[22]

Coming to terms with what the crowd does in American fiction provides, in the most concrete of ways, a context for

21. Barrington Moore states, "Crowds in general are forms of collective human behavior that arise outside of the normal institutional structure, the usual ties of political obedience, obligations to work, and the like. They are holidays from normal society. Like holidays and any form of euphoria (or acute unhappiness) they cannot last. Very soon the imperatives of ordinary life, getting food, exchanging at least some goods and services, reassert themselves." *Injustice: The Social Bases of Obedience and Revolt* (White Plains, N.Y., 1978), 480.

22. Trilling, *The Liberal Imagination*, 206–15, 253–55; Richard Chase, *The American Novel and Its Tradition* (Garden City, 1957), 1–13.

challenging this view. By the very place it fills in American literature, the crowd raises political questions that Trilling and Chase ignore: Where would *The Scarlet Letter* be without Hester's public humiliation before a gathering of her fellow Puritans? How would Ahab continue his hunt for Moby Dick if he did not galvanize his crew around him the way a demagogue galvanizes a mob? What would Huck have to fear in freeing Jim from the Phelpses if there were not a "vigilance committee" of armed farmers ready to spring into action?

But even more telling is the fact that the crowd provides a basis for redefining the meaning of society in American fiction. With the crowd in mind it becomes clear that, if we use the idea of romance to explain what appears to be the social thinness of American fiction, we are overlooking a more basic issue. The American novelist was not interested, as were so many of his Victorian contemporaries, in describing society primarily in terms of class and manners. He had a different and broader agenda. For him the most pressing social questions were ones the crowd constantly raised: Where does ultimate power lie in a democracy? Who dominates whom when established instructions are left behind or lose authority? How do the people of a young nation assert direct control over their political lives? Can they act collectively without at the same time subjecting themselves to the tyranny of mass opinion? These were the issues the American novelist wove into the fabric of his fiction, and if they led him to produce something quite unlike the fiction of Jane Austen, the result was certainly not a novel-romance in which society was tangential. At the very least, it was a brand of fiction in which the politics of the crowd and an obsession with the transcendent were both responses to widespread doubts about the virtues of conventional society.

The irony is that, had the American novelist responded to the crowd in the manner of the English novelists that Trilling and Chase so admire, he would have reduced it to an essentially lower-class phenomenon, and his judgment of it would have been determined by the belief that crowds are so easily inflamed that their character is inherently violent and undemocratic. But by the mid-nineteenth century, the classic American novelists had begun to see their crowd heritage as distinct from that of their European counterparts. The crowd carried a greater range of implication— a larger cast of characters and a different revolutionary tradition—for these writers than for Dickens in *A Tale of Two Cities* or for George Eliot in *Felix Holt* and in turn gave their fiction, like that of the social realists who succeeded them, an engaged quality. Both sets of novelists would find it impossible to describe their fears and hopes for American democracy without also describing a politics in which protests, lynch mobs, and labor strikes were as "natural" as the eighteenth-century uprisings that brought the nation into being and made the crowd so important in the writing of John Adams and Thomas Jefferson.

I

The Revolutionary Crowd of Adams and Jefferson

As the crowd became an increasingly important force in pre-Revolutionary America, the need to explain it—above all, the need to justify crowd action—took on new dimensions. In a divided colony, it was not enough to equate the crowd and the patriot cause. It was also essential to answer the charge that crowd activity menaced the entire social fabric of the colonies—in the words of Thomas Hutchinson, the crowd threatened to "sap the foundation of all government" and create a "*dominatio plebis*" that would end in nothing less than "perfect barbarism."[1]

For the patriots, the great plus was the vision their countrymen already had of the crowd as "the people out-of-doors."[2] A Loyalist such as Peter Oliver might insist, "The people in general . . . were like the mobility of all countries, perfect machines, wound up by any hand who might first take the winch," but the colonists had reason to think otherwise. During the eighteenth century, rioting in America touched both country and city and reflected the fact that for many the crowd was in essence an "extralegal arm" of the community.[3]

1. Thomas Hutchinson quoted in Bernard Bailyn, *The Ordeal of Thomas Hutchinson* (Cambridge, Mass., 1974), 85, 122, 137. See also Pauline Maier, *From Resistance to Revolution* (New York, 1974); Gordon S. Wood, "A Note on Mobs in the American Revolution," *William and Mary Quarterly*, XXIII (October, 1966), 635–42.
2. Gordon S. Wood, *The Creation of the American Republic, 1776–1787* (New York, 1972), 319–21. See also Rhys Isaac, "Dramatizing the Ideology of the Revolution: Popular Mobilization in Virginia, 1774 to 1776," *William and Mary Quarterly*, XXXIII (July, 1976), 357–85.
3. Douglass Adair and John A. Schutz (eds.), *Peter Oliver's Origin and Progress of the American Revolution* (San Marino, Calif., 1961), 65; Pauline Maier, "Popular Uprisings and Civil Authority in Eighteenth-Century America," *William and Mary Quarterly*, XXVII (January, 1970), 3–5.

In the decade prior to the revolution, the crowd was instrumental in causing stamp agents to resign, obstructing the enforcement of the Townshend Acts, and effecting a boycott of British goods. The precedents for such anti-imperial action had been established many years earlier when crowds intervened to keep foodstuffs in the colony during periods of famine, to stop impressment, and to challenge the White Pines Acts. Indeed, by the time of the Revolution, crowd action was sufficiently widespread and organized that on numerous occasions it not only had broad support but benefited from the direct involvement of artisans, shopkeepers, and workmen, and from the behind-the-scenes guidance of some of the most prominent families in America.[4]

The colonial crowd could not be dismissed as a mark of New World political immaturity. Well before 1776, the crowd was an established fact of European social and economic life. In the 1640s the intervention of the crowd in the politics of the Long Parliament was decisive in bringing about the defeat of the king, lords, and bishops. And in the half century before the American Revolution, food riots, in which crowds sought to regulate grain prices and correct what they believed were unfair practices in marketing, milling, and baking, were commonplace in England. Such activity did not go unnoticed by the colonists, who from the early seventeenth century on constantly had their eyes on the mother country. In the 1780s, even so circumspect a politician as John Jay could not help comparing the English and American crowd. "These People," Jay wrote of Daniel Shays's followers, "bear no resemblance to an English Mob—they are more temperate, cool and regular in their conduct—they have hitherto abstained from Plunder, nor have they that I know committed any outrages but such as the accomplishment of their purpose made necessary."[5]

4. Bernard Bailyn (ed.), *Pamphlets of the American Revolution, 1750–1776* (Cambridge, Mass., 1965), 581–84; Maier, "Popular Uprisings," 5–15; Jesse Lemisch, "Jack Tar in the Streets: Merchant Seamen in the Politics of Revolutionary America," *William and Mary Quarterly*, XXV (July, 1968), 371–407; Edmund Morgan and Helen Morgan, *The Stamp Act Crisis: Prelude to Revolution* (Chapel Hill, 1953), 180–92.

5. Brian Manning, *The English People and the English Revolution, 1640–49* (London, 1976), 1–70; E. P. Thompson, "The Moral Economy of the English Crowd in the Eighteenth Century," *Past and Present*, L (February, 1971),

In their analyses of the crowd, John Adams and Thomas Jefferson were both aware of and influenced by these favoring historical winds. They were too much the consummate politicians not to be. Yet what they have to say about the crowd is not merely intended to serve the patriot cause or, for that matter, to be self-serving and reflect the mixed feelings they had about the crowd as a political force. Their writing on the crowd is more far-reaching than that. It is both politically timeless, designed to speak to what Adams called the "immutable, eternal foundation" of revolution, and at the same time extraordinarily sensitive to matters of style. As Peter Shaw notes in his *American Patriots and the Rituals of Revolution,* the "expressive behavior" and "ritual symbolism" employed by patriot crowds during the 1760s and 1770s often proved more important than their actual deeds.[6]

Adams' and Jefferson's writings on the crowd, especially their letters and diaries, may thus be approached as we would a novel or an autobiography in which the elements of composition—tone, imagery, point of view, and structure—are as crucial as the formal subject matter. We may indeed go a step further and say that Adams' and Jefferson's writings on the crowd must be looked at in these terms if we are to realize that America has a rich and complex eighteenth-century crowd literature, not merely a plethora of eighteenth-century pamphlets and position papers that deal with the crowd.[7]

For John Adams, direct, personal involvement with crowds was always something he felt uneasy about. "Large and pro-

---

76–136; George Rudé, *The Crowd in History* (New York, 1964), 33–65; John Jay to Thomas Jefferson, December 14, 1786, in Julian P. Boyd, Lyman H. Butterfield, and Mina R. Bryan (eds.), *The Papers of Thomas Jefferson* (21 vols.; Princeton, 1950–82), X, 597.

6. John Adams to H. Niles, February 13, 1818, in Charles Francis Adams (ed.), *The Works of John Adams* (10 vols.; Boston, 1850–56), X, 283; Peter Shaw, *American Patriots and the Rituals of Revolution* (Cambridge, Mass., 1981), 5–25. See also Jefferson to Judge John Tyler, June 28, 1804, in Philip Foner (ed.), *Basic Writings of Thomas Jefferson* (New York, 1944), 667; Adams to Thomas Jefferson, February 2, 1816, in Lester J. Cappon (ed.), *The Adams-Jefferson Letters* (2 vols.; Chapel Hill, 1959), II, 463.

7. For a discussion of style in the pamphlets of the American Revolution, see Bernard Bailyn, *The Ideological Origins of the American Revolution* (Cambridge, Mass., 1967), 1–21.

miscuous companies" of any sort were obnoxious to him. Of all the revolutionary leaders, however, Adams has the most to say about the crowd and is the most enigmatic in that regard as well. Nothing is more evident from his writings than his belief that the crowd (which he often described as a mob even when he did not mean to classify it as such) was always dangerous. "It is sometimes said, that mobs are a good mode of expressing the sense, the resentments, the feelings of the people," he wrote in 1778. "But if the principle is once admitted, liberty and the rights of mankind will invariably be betrayed; for it is giving liberty to tories and courtiers to excite mobs as well as to patriots." The closer we look at Adams' writings, however, the more apparent it becomes that his apprehension about crowds is a starting, not a finishing, point. He was, for example, painfully aware that those who opposed the patriot cause were not above equating it with mob rule, and he had great contempt for ministers' glib moralizing on the subject of the mob. A year before the outbreak of war with England, he wrote Abigail:

> Mobs are the trite Topick of Declamation and Invective, among all the ministerial People, far and near. They are grown universally learned in the Nature, Tendency and Consequences of them, and very eloquent and pathetic in descanting upon them. They are Sources of all kinds of Evils, Vices, and Crimes, they say. . . . Besides, they render the Populace, the Rabble, the scum of the Earth, insolent, and disorderly, impudent, and abusive. . . .
>
> This is the Picture drawn by the Tory Pencil: and it must be granted to be a Likeness; but this is Declamation. What Consequence is to be drawn from this Description? Shall We submit to Parliamentary Taxation, to avoid Mobs? Will not Parliamentary Taxation, if established, occasion Vices, Crimes and Follies, infinitely more numerous, dangerous, and fatal to the Community?[8]

Adams also believed that crowds could exercise popular justice and do so in a reasonable, if rough, manner. In the summer of 1777, Abigail could entertain him with "an account of

8. Adams to Mercy Warren, November 25, 1775, and Adams, "Defence of the Constitution of Government of the United States of America," both in C. F. Adams (ed.), *Works*, IX, 368, V, 456–57; Adams to Abigail Adams, July 6, 1774, in L. H. Butterfield, Wendell D. Garrett, and Marjorie E. Sprague (eds.), *Adams Family Correspondence* (4 vols.; Cambridge, Mass., 1963–1973), I, 126.

a New Set of Mobility"—a group of women who attacked "an eminent, wealthy, stingy Merchant" (Thomas Boylston) when he refused to sell his coffee for what they believed was a fair price.

> You must know that there is a great Scarcity of Sugar and Coffe, articles which the Female part of the State are very loth to give up, expecially whilst they consider the Scarcity occasioned by the merchants having secreted a large Quantity. . . . A number of Females some say a hundred, some say more . . . marched down to the [Boylston] Ware House and demanded the keys, which he re-fused to deliver, upon which one of them seazd him by his Neck and tossed him into the cart. Upon his finding no Quarter he delivered the keys, when they tipd up the cart and dischargd him, then opend the Warehouse, Hoisted out the Coffe themselves, put it into the trucks and drove off. . . . A large concourse of Men stood amazd silent Spectators of the whole transaction.[9]

To fully understand Adams' writings on crowds, we must look closely at the emphasis he placed on the circumstances from which crowds arose, and for this task the best and most obvious starting point is the Boston Massacre of 1770. A half century after its occurrence, Adams was still writing about it in his letters, and his comments reflect the principles he used throughout his life for judging crowds.

Adams' decision to act as defense counsel for the British troops who had fired on and killed Boston citizens caused him great anguish. Two years after the trial, he refused to give the annual Massacre Day address because he felt that the role he had taken still made him subject "to the Lash of ignorant and malicious Tongues." And as late as 1809, he complained to Benjamin Rush, "My sense of equity and humanity impelled me, against a torrent of unpopularity, and the inclinations of all my friends, to engage in the defence of Captain Preston and the soldiers. My successful exertions . . . brought upon me a load of indignation and unpopularity, which I knew would never be forgotten, nor entirely forgiven."[10]

Adams' defense of Preston and the British soldiers was not,

9. Abigail Adams to John Adams, July 31, 1777, in Butterfield, Garrett, and Sprague (eds.), *Family Correspondence*, II, 295.

10. John Adams, "Diary," December 29, 1772, in L. H. Butterfield, Leonard C. Faber, Wendell D. Garrett (eds.), *Diary and Autobiography of John Adams*

however, undertaken naïvely (he was in Boston on the night of the Massacre and followed an angry crowd to the scene of the action). When we look at his "Massacre Notes," written during the trial, and at his *Autobiography*, written many years later, what emerges is a view of the crowd that offers implicit and explicit revolutionary standards of judgment. That Adams believed he was judging the Massacre crowd by standards that would support a democratic revolution is especially evident in his *Autobiography*, where his real worry is that the crowd acted prematurely and drew attention away from the larger issue of British occupation. Particularly "disquieting" to Adams were three facts: the Massacre crowd was "lower class" and unrepresentative of the population; it lacked political sophistication and was easily manipulated; and there was no certainty that the country as a whole would support such direct confrontations with the British.

My Wife having heard that the Town was still and likely to continue so, had recovered from her first Apprehensions, and We had nothing but our Reflections to interrupt our Repose. These Reflections were to me, disquieting enough. Endeavors had been systematically pursued for many Months, by certain busy Characters, to excite Quarrells, Rencounters and Combats single or compound in the night between in Inhabitants of the lower Class and the Soldiers, and at all risques to inkindle an immortal hatred between them. I suspected that this was the Explosion which had been intentionally wrought up by designing Men, who knew what they were aiming at better than the Instrument employed. If these poor Tools should be prosecuted for any of their illegal Conduct they must be punished. If the Soldiers in self defence should kill any of them they must be tryed, and if Truth was respected and the Law prevailed must be acquitted. . . . It would be better for the whole People to rise in their Majesty, and insist on the removal of the Army, and take upon themselves the Consequences, than to excite such Passions between the People and the Soldiers as would expose both to continual prosecution civil or criminal and keep the Town boiling in a continual formentation. The real and full Intentions of the British Government and Nation were not yet developed: and We knew not whether the Town would be supported by

---

(4 vols.; Cambridge, Mass., 1961), II, 74; Adams to Benjamin Rush, April 12, 1809, in C. F. Adams (ed.), *Works*, IX, 616–17.

the Country . . . nor whether New England would be supported by the Continent.[11]

Adams' "Massacre Notes," written thirty-four years earlier, reflects, in a more systematic fashion, the same view of the crowd. In his address to the jury, Adams carefully analyzed the aims, the conduct, and the composition of the Massacre crowd, and did so with the explicit proviso that there were occasions when crowd action was "warranted." Anyone hearing Adams speak that day would have had difficulty ignoring the revolutionary implications of his address. Tumults and insurrections were, Adams pointed out to the jury (with imagery designed to merge the natural and the political), inherent in society and generally in proportion to the despotism of a government:

> In the continual vicissitudes of human things . . . the people are liable to run into riots and tumults. There are Church-quakes and state-quakes in the moral and political world, as well as earthquakes, storms, and tempests in the physical. This much however must be said in favor of the people and human nature, that it is a general, if not universal truth, that the aptitude of the people to mutinies, seditions, and tumults and insurrections, is in direct proportion to the despotism of the government.

Equally important, there were British practices, such as impressment, that made it justifiable for a crowd to take the law into its hands.

> Suppose a press gang should come on shore in this town and assault any sailor or householder in *King street,* in order to carry them on board one of his Majesty's ships . . . would not the inhabitants think themselves warranted by law to interpose in behalf of their fellow citizens? . . . I believe we shall not have it disputed, that it would be lawful to go into *King-street* and help an honest man there against the press master.

The problem, Adams told the jury, was that no such issue was at stake here. There was no way "to apply the word rebel on this occasion." What characterized those who attacked Preston's troops was primarily a desire to provoke and to maim.

11. Adams, "Autobiography," in Butterfield, Faber, and Garrett (eds.), *Diary and Autobiography,* III, 292.

The situation the British troops were confronted with was one in which "the multitude was shouting and huzzaing, and threatening life, the bells all ringing, the mob whistle screaming and rending like an Indian yell, the people from all quarters throwing every species of rubbish they could pick up in the street."[12]

What more was there to say of such "poor Tools"? As far as Adams was concerned, only that they were unrepresentative of Boston and not the kind of men around whom one built a revolution:

> We have been entertained with a great variety of phrases to avoid calling this sort of people a mob.—Some call them shavers, some call them genius's.—The plain English is gentlemen, most probably a rabble of saucy boys, negroes and molattoes, Irish teagues and out landish jack tarrs. And why should we scruple to call such a set of people a mob, I can't conceive, unless the name is too respectable for them.

Years later, when in the public mind the Boston Massacre would assume the status of a revolutionary event, Adams would describe it in much more favorable terms, insisting, "Not the battle of Lexington or Bunker Hill, nor the surrender of Burgoyne or Cornwallis were more important events in American history than the battle of King Street, on the 5th of March, 1770." Yet, in this sanitized version of the Massacre, Adams did not alter his judgment of the crowd itself. What he noted as important here and in succeeding years was the effect of the crowd: "the death of four or five persons, the most obscure and inconsiderable that could have been found upon the continent" touched the population as a whole, with the result that after "the melancholy catastrophe" there "appeared the spirit of freemen; multitudes from Boston and the neighboring towns assembled spontaneously the next day, and from day to day."[13]

12. *Rex* v. *Wemms*, in L. Kinvin Wroth and Hiller B. Zobel (eds.), *Legal Papers of John Adams* (3 vols.; Cambridge, Mass., 1965), III, 249–50, 253, 252, 268.
13. *Ibid.*, 266; Adams to J. Morse, January 5, 1816, Adams to James Burgh, December 28, 1774, Adams to J. Morse, January 1, 1816, all in C. F. Adams (ed.), *Works*, X, 203, IX, 352, X, 200.

When we examine Adams' later reactions to crowds, we see them still structured by the ideas he articulated at the time of the Boston Massacre—namely, that for a crowd to be a significant, progressive force it must be disciplined in its conduct and have clear aims, represent the population as a whole, arise as a last resort, and stem from a situation in which nothing short of crowd action will do. The conservatism so often noted as dominating Adams' politics from 1780 on may have changed specific observations he made about crowds, but it did not change the standards he used in judging them or his belief that the disorder of a "tumultuous" people was preferable to tyranny "provided there was any hope that the fair order of liberty and a free constitution would arise out of it." [14] When we look at the letters and political documents Adams wrote in the period between the Boston Tea Party and the French Revolution, we see a remarkably consistent, though increasingly unhappy, student of crowds.

Even on the cusp of the American Revolution, Adams did not hesitate to oppose patriotic crowd violence when he thought it personal, not political, in thrust. In July, 1774, he took up the case of Richard King, a Maine resident whose store and home had been attacked eight years earlier when he was suspected of being a prospective Stamp Act officer. For Adams it was a less costly but more impolitic decision than his defense of the Boston Massacre soldiers. What emerges in the letter he wrote Abigail following the King trial is not, however, concern for himself but passionate sympathy for King and absolute fury at the mob that broke into King's house. Adams' fury is again coupled with an explanation of when crowd action—"Popular Commotions," as Adams calls it here—is appropriate:

> I am engaged in a famous Cause: The Cause of King, of Scarborough vs. a Mob, that broke into his House, and rifled his Papers, and terrifyed him, his Wife, Children and Servants in the Night. The Terror, and Distress, the Distraction and Horror of this Family cannot be described by Words or painted upon Canvess. . . . These private Mobs, I do and will detest. If popular Commotions can be justi-

14. Adams, "Defence of the Constitution of Government of the United States of America," in C. F. Adams (ed.), *Works*, VI, 151. See also John R. Howe, Jr., *The Changing Political Thought of John Adams* (Princeton, 1966), 146–48.

fyed, in Opposition to Attacks upon the Constitution, it can be only when Fundamentals are invaded, nor then unless for absolute Necessity and with great Caution. But these Tarrings and Featherings, these breaking open Houses by rude and insolent Rabbles, in Resentment for private Wrongs or in pursuance of private Prejudices and Passions must be discountenanced.[15]

Adams' defense of King becomes even more telling when we remember that at this time he was doing anything but waiting for the ideal revolutionary crowd to appear and act. The standards he had set up earlier for judging crowds were working standards, and his response to the Boston Tea Party bears that out. It would certainly have been possible for Adams to have had second thoughts about a group of men dressed as Indians and followed by a crowd, going aboard a ship in Boston harbor and throwing its cargo overboard. There is logic as well as Tory rhetoric in Daniel Leonard's description of the Tea Party as "a more unaccountable frenzy and more disgraceful to the annals of America, than that of witchcraft." Yet, as far as Adams was concerned, the Tea Party was nothing less than "magnificent." In his *Diary* entry for December 17, 1773, his joy is unmistakable:

> Last night 3 Cargoes of Bohes Tea were emptied into the Sea. This Morning a Man of War sails.
> This is the most magnificent Movement of all. There is a Dignity, a Majesty, a Sublimity, in this last Effort of the Patriots, that I greatly admire. The People should never rise, without doing something to be remembered—something notable. And striking. This Destruction of the Tea is so bold, so daring, so firm, intrepid and inflexible . . . that I cant but consider it as an Epoch in History.

In terms of Adams and the crowd, what is especially worth noting is how thoroughly his enthusiasm for the Tea Party crowd is spelled out. In Adams' eyes, it is the embodiment of "popular Power" exercised in a "notable" and "lasting" fashion, yet free from the "destruction of lives." As far as Adams was concerned, the British had only themselves to blame for the Tea Party:

> The Question is whether the Destruction of this Tea was necessary? I apprehend it was absolutely and indispensably so.—They

15. Wroth and Zobel (eds.), *Legal Papers*, I, 106, 140.

could not send it back, the Governor, Admiral and Collector and Comptroller would not suffer it. It was in their Power to have saved it—but in no other. . . . To let it be landed . . . was losing all our labor for 10 years and subjecting ourselves and our Posterity forever to Egyptian Taskmasters—to Burthens, Indignities, to Ignominy, Reproach and Contempt, to Desolation and Oppression, to Poverty and Servitude.[16]

For the rest of the 1770s, particularly in his "Novanglus" essays of 1775, Adams continued to develop this position. Although he never came up with a vocabulary precisely suited to his needs, Adams began to make increasingly fine judgments of crowd activity. He insisted that revolutionary crowd action supported by the people—whom he defined in Pufendorf's terms as "the greater and more judicious part of the subjects of all ranks"—could not be classified as a riot. "None were indicted for pulling down a stamp office," he observed in defending the decision of a colonial jury, "because this was thought to be an honorable and glorious action, not a riot." By the same token, British authorities could justly be accused of acting like a mob. In words that suggest the modern idea of a police riot, Adams argued that "the worst sorts of tumults and outrages ever committed in this province were excited by the tories." It was certain, he noted, "that mobs have been thought a necessary ingredient by the tories in their system of administration, mobs of the worst sort, with red coats, fuzees, and bayonets."[17]

It is not until the 1780s and his diplomatic stay in Europe that we find the tone of Adams' writings on the crowd changing and his taking less comfort than before in his observation that "seditious proceedings from malice are seldom or never seen in popular government." News of the Gordon Riots in London during June, 1780, left Adams filled with horror. As he wrote Abigail, it was little compensation to discover that the rioters were pro-American:

London is in the Horrors. Governor Hutchinson fell down dead at the first appearance of Mobs. They have been terrible. A Spirit of

16. Daniel Leonard quoted in Page Smith, *John Adams* (2 vols.; Garden City, 1962), I, 149; Adams, "Diary," December 17, 1773, in Butterfield, Faber, and Garrett (eds.), *Diary and Autobiography,* II, 85–86.
17. Adams, "Novanglus," in C. F. Adams (ed.), *Works,* IV, 82, 74, 57, 52.

Bigotry and Fanaticism, mixing with the universal discontents of the nation was broken out into Violences of the most dreadful Nature—burnt Lord Mansfield's House, Books, Manuscripts—burnd the Kings Bench Prison, and all the other Prisons. . . . And where it will end God only knows.—The Mobs all cryd Peace with America, and War with France—poor Wretches! as if this were possible.

The greatest shock for Adams in this period, however, was Shays's Rebellion of 1786. This uprising by farmers in western Massachusetts, who, under the leadership of a former Revolutionary War officer, sought to have their taxes lowered and to stop creditors from taking action against their farms, presented Adams with a difficult problem. At the outset he could minimize the importance of their rebellion, as he did when he wrote Jefferson, "Don't be alarmed at the late Turbulence in New England. The Massachusetts Assembly had, in its zeal to get the better of their debt, laid on a tax rather heavier than the People could bear, but it will be well, and this Commotion will terminate in additional Strength to Government." It was not possible for Adams to maintain this position for long, however. In her correspondence with Jefferson, Abigail sounded the note the Adamses were finally to take with regard to the rebellion.

With regard to the Tumults in my Native state. . . . Ignorant, wrestless desperadoes without conscience or principals, have led a deluded multitude to follow their standard, under pretense of grievances, which have no existence but in their imaginations. Some of them were crying out for a paper currency, some for an equal distribution of property, some were for annihilating all debts. . . . By this list you will see the materials which compose this rebellion, and the necessity there is of the wisest and most vigorous measures to quell and suppress it. . . . These mobbish insurgents are for sapping the foundation, and destroying the whole fabrick at once.[18]

We are at this point a long way from the geographic and nationalistic optimism Adams felt in 1775 when he concluded "Novanglus" with the observation that in a country like Amer-

18. *Ibid.*, 80; Adams to Abigail Adams, June 17, 1780, in Butterfield, Garrett, and Sprague (eds.), *Family Correspondence*, III, 366–67; Adams to Thomas Jefferson, November 30, 1786, Abigail Adams to Thomas Jefferson, January 29, 1787, both in Cappon (ed.), *Adams-Jefferson Letters*, I, 156, 168.

ica with "a people living chiefly by agriculture, in small numbers, sprinkled over large tracts of land," there is little danger
of those "contagions of madness and folly, which are seen in
countries where large numbers live in small places, in daily
fear of perishing for want."[19] Yet the closer we look at the
standards Abigail used to condemn Shays's rebels, the more
apparent it becomes that they are in essence a replica of those
John used earlier to criticize the Boston Massacre crowd. To
Abigail, the Shaysites are not disciplined men but a "deluded
multitude." They do not represent the nation but are "ignorant, wrestless desperadoes," and their action is not a revolutionary last resort so much as an effort to serve their own interests—to the point of seeking "an equal distribution of
property" in some cases.

For his part, John expressed no uneasiness over Abigail's
view of Shays's Rebellion, and later went out of his way to insist on the consistency of his own thinking on the matter.
"Mobs will never do to govern states or command armies. I
was as sensible of it in 1770 as I am in 1787," he wrote Benjamin Hichborn. "To talk of liberty in such a state of things! Is
not a Shattuck or Shays as great a tyrant . . . as a Bernard or
Hutchinson?" The problem for Adams was that from 1786 on,
being consistent would turn out to mean being in opposition
to most crowds. It was perfectly logical for him to sum up his
feelings about Shays's Rebellion by concluding, "The just
complaints of the people of real grievances ought never to
be discouraged and even their imaginary grievances may be
treated with too great severity. But when a cry is set up for the
abolition of debts, equal distribution of property, and the abolition of senators and governors, it is time for every honest
man to consider his situation." In the past Adams had always
opposed leveling and the pitting of the haves against the have-
nots. Long before the Revolution, he had complained to Abigail
of those who thought the "politest and genteelist" were on
the side of the administration and the "Multitude, the Vulgar,
the Herd, the Rabble" were the primary supporters of the patriot cause.[20]

19. Adams, "Novanglus," in C. F. Adams (ed.), *Works*, IV, 587.
20. Adams to Benjamin Hichborn, January 27, 1787, in C. F. Adams (ed.),
Works, IX, 551; Adams to John Jay, November 30, 1786, in Smith, *John*

As time went on, however, Adams' fears of leveling only made him seem more conservative than ever. In public he came across as a man whose concern with class had come to dominate all his other interests. It was a situation that left him no way out, and when we look at Adams' final writings on the crowd, we see his awareness of his own predicament. He does not curry favor. He attacks Edmund Burke for his use of "swinish multitude" as a label for the people of a country, but he also attacks those revolutionaries who "pant for equality of persons and property." It is an accepting, rather than bitter Adams who writes Jefferson:

> When I saw that Shaises Rebellion was breaking out in Massachusetts, and when I saw that even my obscure Name was often quoted in France as an Advocate for simple Democracy; when I saw that the Sympathies in America had caught the French flame: I was determined to wash my own hands as clean as I could of all this foulness. I had then strong forebodings that I was sacrificing all the honours and Emoluments of this Life; and so it has happened: but not in so great a degree as I apprehended. . . . Your steady defence of democratical Principles and your invariable favourable Opinion of the French Revolution laid the foundation of your Unbounded Popularity.
>
> Sic transit Gloria Mundi.[21]

As far as Adams was concerned, the French Revolution was the source of the first serious political disagreement between himself and Jefferson. Adams made this point to Benjamin Rush in 1811, adding, "I know of no difference between him and myself relative to the Constitution, or to forms of government in general," and it was a point he repeated two years later to Jefferson. "The first time that you and I differed in Opinion on any material Question was; after your Arrival from Europe; and that point was the French Revolution," he stated. If we are to understand Jefferson on the crowd, particularly in re-

---

Adams, II, 690; Adams to Abigail Adams, July 7, 1774, in Butterfield, Garrett, and Sprague (eds.), *Family Correspondence,* I, 130.

21. Adams, "Letters to John Taylor of Caroline in Reply to his Strictures on Some Parts of the Defence of the American Constitutions," Adams to Richard Price, April 19, 1790, both in C. F. Adams (ed.), *Works,* VI, 496, IX, 564; Adams to Thomas Jefferson, July 13, 1813, in Cappon (ed.), *Adams-Jefferson Letters,* II, 356.

lation to Adams, we must, however, start with a less chari-
table observation Adams made when he wrote Jefferson:

> You never felt the Terrorism of Chaises Rebellion in Massachu-
> setts. I believe you never felt the Terrorism of Gallatins Insurrec-
> tion in Pensilvania. You certainly never realized the Terrorism of
> Fries's, most outrageous Riot and Rescue. . . . You certainly never
> felt the Terrorism, excited by Genet in 1793, when ten thousand
> People in the Streets of Philadelphia, day after day, threatened to
> drag Washington out of his House, and effect a Revolution in Gov-
> ernment, or compell it to declare War in favor of the French Revo-
> lution, and aginst England. . . . You was fast asleep in philosophi-
> cal Tranquility, when ten thousand People, and perhaps many
> more, were parading the Streets of Philadelphia, on the Evening of
> my Fast Day.[22]

Adams' charges point to the fact that by the middle 1780s,
Jefferson feared that minor disorders in the country would
lead to a series of harsh governmental reactions. As a result,
his instinct was to downplay the dangers of an uprising such
as Shays's Rebellion. In the letters he wrote on the rebellion,
Jefferson keeps coming back to the point that an aroused
people have a role to play in the normal course of government
as well as during revolution. He is convinced that in America
the dangers of "tumults" are limited by the "good sense of the
people," who "may be led astray for a moment, but will soon
correct themselves." When Abigail Adams goes out of her way
to tell him of the threat posed by the "mad cry of the mob,"
Jefferson dismisses her long and pained description of Shays's
Rebellion in a few sentences. "The spirit of resistance to government is so valuable on certain occasions, that I wish it to
be always kept alive," he writes. "It will often be exercised
when wrong, but better so than not to be exercised at all. I
like a little rebellion now and then. It is like a storm in the
Atmosphere." Nor is Abigail Adams the only one Jefferson
writes in this spirit. With James Madison he adopts the same
imagery and the same tone, first insisting that "a little rebellion now and then" is "as necessary in the political world as
storms in the physical," then adding that "honest republican

22. Adams to Benjamin Rush, December 25, 1811, in C. F. Adams (ed.),
Works, X, 10; Adams to Thomas Jefferson, July 13, 1813, June 30, 1813, both
in Cappon (ed.), *Adams-Jefferson Letters*, II, 354–55, 346–47.

governors" should try "not to discourage them too much."
With William Smith, John Adams' son-in-law, Jefferson cannot
resist answering his own rhetorical questions about Shays's
Rebellion with a burst of hyperbole: "And can history produce
an instance of rebellion so honorably conducted? . . . What sig-
nify a few lives lost in a century or two?" he asks. After all,
"The tree of liberty must be refreshed from time to time with
the blood of patriots and tyrants. It is its natural manure."[23]

The irony is that despite the impression his comments on
Shays's Rebellion give, and despite his disagreements with
Adams on the French Revolution, Jefferson was much like
Adams in his overall approach to crowds. For judging them, he
used essentially the same framework, albeit often with different results. The representativeness of a crowd, its aims and in-
ternal discipline, its emergence as a democratic last resort
were all crucial to Jefferson. Where Jefferson's writings depart
from Adams'—and extend their range—is in the emphasis he
came to place on the faces and life of a crowd.

Jefferson's letters on the French Revolution best illustrate
this difference, but to see these letters in perspective, we must
take a second and longer look at his writings on the crowd in
America. Here we find an approach to the crowd that is both
cautious in nature and inseparable from Jefferson's sense of
the historical uniqueness of America. For Jefferson, the crucial fact is that the body politic of America is far healthier
than that of Europe. "Those who labor in the earth are the
chosen people of God, if ever He had a chosen people, whose
breasts he made His peculiar deposit for substantial and genuine virtue," he writes in *Notes on the State of Virginia*, and
then goes on to observe that in contrast to land-rich America,
Europe is faced with a situation in which "the mobs of the
great cities add so much to the support of pure government, as
sores do to the human body." In an underpopulated America,
Jefferson did not worry, as his friend Madison did in *The Federalist*, over that "unhappy species of population . . . who,
during the calm of regular government, are sunk below the

23. Maier, "Popular Uprisings," 26; Jefferson to Edward Carrington, January 16, 1787, Jefferson to Abigail Adams, February 22, 1787, Jefferson to James
Madison, January 30, 1787, Jefferson to William Smith, November 13, 1787,
all in Boyd, Butterfield, and Bryan (eds.), *Papers*, XI, 49, 174, 93, XII, 356.

level of men; but who in tempestuous scenes of civil violence, may . . . give a superiority of strength to any party with which they may associate themselves."[24]

In the 1770s and 1780s, Jefferson was thus able to praise and to criticize the crowd in America with a great deal of assurance. On one hand, he could support the actions of those who "assembled in the town of Boston" and "threw the tea into the ocean" with the simple observation, "There are extraordinary situations which require extraordinary interposition. An exasperated people, who feel that they possess power, are not easily restrained within limits strictly regular." On the other hand, he could provide a correspondent like William Carmichael with a detailed account of a vicious New York riot in which a mob, suspecting several doctors of grave robbing, attacked the prison in which they took asylum, and the "militia, thinking the mob had just provocation, refused to turn out." As far as Jefferson was concerned, neither the Tea Party nor the New York riot, which he feared might be "represented as a political riot, when politics had nothing to do with it," threatened to ignite the kind of social upheaval that would bring to power the equivalent of a European working class.[25]

A closer look at Jefferson's comments on Shays's Rebellion makes his accepting view of the American crowd all the more clear. We see that Jefferson's observations on the rebellion, even when they seem most supportive, are not dependent on his approval of the rebels or their specific cause. They acted "in ignorance," he tells William Smith. It is "most probably" that they were of "the imprudent number" who have "involved themselves in debt beyond their abilities to pay," he writes David Hartley. What makes Jefferson willing to defend such "turbulence" and "rebellion" on the part of the people is his belief that their protests are therapeutic, "a medicine necessary for the sound health of government."

I am persuaded myself that the good sense of the people will always found to be the best army. They may be led astray for a mo-

24. Thomas Jefferson, *Notes on the State of Virginia* (New York, 1964), 57–58; James Madison, "Federalist No. 43," in *The Federalist* (New York, n.d.), 285.
25. Thomas Jefferson, "A Summary View 1774," Jefferson to William Carmichael, June 3, 1788, both in Boyd, Butterfield, and Bryan (eds.), *Papers*, I, 127, XIII, 233.

ment, but will soon correct themselves. The people are the only censors of their governors: and even their errors will tend to keep these to the true principles of their institutions. To punish these errors too severely would be to suppress the only safeguard of the public liberty.[26]

Jefferson's writings on the French Revolution, minus his pro-American, pro-agrarian feelings, reflect this same pragmatic faith in the people and the crowd as the best defense against a despotic government. Indeed, nothing is more characteristic of Jefferson's thinking at this time than its practical orientation. In Paris, Jefferson is, for all his concern with the drafting of the *Declaration of the Rights of Man*, wholly unwilling to play the role of uncompromising ideologue and revolutionary. With such friends as the Marquis de Lafayette, he is the constant advocate of a political "middle ground." At one point he suggests "placing the privileged classes together in one house and the unprivileged in another" to avoid a "scission," and at another point urges that "in a *seance royale*" the King offer "a charter containing all the good in which all parties agree."[27] Jefferson's overall observations on the crowd in the French Revolution combine the same restraint and practicality. When he was confronted with actual crowd violence, Jefferson's humane and cautious instincts took over. He was anxious for as little blood as possible to be spilled, and his prose reflects this desire. He is constantly noting and praising the restraint of the revolutionary crowds of Paris. He describes them as "the people" rather than a faction or rabble, and whenever possible, he depicts them as being forced into violence, not initiating it or overreacting to violence forced upon them.

The emphasis Jefferson placed on portraying the faces and subjective life of the French revolutionary crowd makes his perspective all the more clear. Jefferson is terribly self-conscious about his on-the-scene observations. Time and again his letters focus on the variety and scope of the French crowds' actions and on the need for having direct insight into them. His

26. Jefferson to William Smith, November 13, 1787, Jefferson to David Hartley, July 2, 1787, Jefferson to James Madison, January 30, 1787, Jefferson to Edward Carrington, January 16, 1787, all in *ibid.*, XII, 356, XI, 526, 93, 49.
27. Jefferson to Lafayette, May 6, 1789, Jefferson to Lafayette, June 3, 1789, both in *ibid.*, XV, 98, 165.

comment to Adams in 1791 that his faith in the French Revolution "always rested on my own ocular evidence" is amply borne out by the letters he wrote during 1789. Jefferson rarely allows his friends to forget that he saw or had direct knowledge from an eyewitness of scenes "too interesting to be left," and he is constantly supplying them with details that establish his presence in Paris.[28] The point Jefferson wants to make above all others is that to cut through rumor and half-truths, an active narrator-observer, not an armchair historian, is needed. Jefferson's sense of his own reportorial role appears in a letter written to John Jay five days after the fall of the Bastille.

> I went yesterday to Versailles to satisfy myself what had passed there; for nothing can be believed but what one sees, or has from an eye-witness. They believe still that 3000 people have fallen victims to the tumults of Paris. [But] Mr. Short and myself have been every day among them in order to be sure of what was passing. We cannot find with certainty that any body has been killed but the three before-mentioned and those who fell in the assault or defence of the Bastille.[29]

The result of this eyewitnessing is that for Jefferson, the French revolutionary crowd is never an undifferentiated mass. When he evaluates it in terms of the standards Adams used to judge the crowd in America—that is, in terms of its representativeness, its discipline and aims, and its emergence as a political last resort—the conclusions he reaches are overwhelmingly favorable. By 1789, Jefferson has in fact become more convinced than ever that the Paris crowds are a legitimate political force and that without their taking to the streets the government could not be significantly changed.

> I have . . . observed the mobs with my own eyes in order to be satisfied of their objects, and declare to you that I saw so plainly the legitimacy of them, that I have slept in my house as quietly thro' the whole as I ever did in the most peaceable moments. So strongly

28. Jefferson to John Adams, August 30, 1791, in Cappon (ed.), Adams-Jefferson Letters, I, 251–52; Jefferson to John Jay, July 19, 1789, in Boyd, Butterfield, and Bryan (eds.), Papers, XV, 289. On Jefferson as eyewitness to the French Revolution, see Howard C. Rice, Jr., Thomas Jefferson's Paris (Princeton, 1976), 118.
29. Jefferson to John Jay, July 19, 1789, in Boyd, Butterfield, and Bryan (eds.), Papers, XV, 290.

fortified was the despotism of this government by long possession, by the respect and fears of the people . . . the national assembly with all their good sense, could without mobs probably have only obtained a considerable improvement of the government, not a total revision of it.[30]

Even the composition of the Paris crowds, a source of anxiety for so many observers of the Revolution, is not off-putting for Jefferson. He constantly describes them as "the people," and in doing so he has at least two objectives. In negative terms he wants to distinguish the crowd from the rabble, those he regards as "the Canaille of the cities of Europe." In positive terms he wants to point out that the representativeness of the French revolutionary crowd is often less a matter of their embodying all classes than of their being in harmony with and advancing the revolutionary "unanimity of the nation." The following tableau, done on the grand scale of David, Jefferson's favorite Paris artist, brings out Jefferson's feelings about the French crowd in a way that no abstract analysis by him of class interests could. The crowd, shown here surrounding the king after his ministers have been fired, is significant not because it has absorbed all classes (Lafayette and others stand out) but because it is at the center of an action in which everyone has put aside his differences for the sake of the Revolution.

Omitting the less important figures of the procession, I will only observe that the king's carriage was in the center, on each side of it the States general, in two ranks, afoot, at their head the Marquis de la Fayette as commander in chief, on horseback, and Bourgeois guards before and behind. About 60,000 citizens of all forms and colors, armed with the muskets of the Bastille and Invalids as far as they would go, the rest with pistols, swords, pikes, pruning hooks, scythes & c. lined all the streets thro' which the procession passed, and, with the crowds of people in the streets, doors, and windows, saluted them every where with cries of "vive la nation."[31]

30. Jefferson to Diodati, August 3, 1789, in *Ibid.*, 325–26.

31. Jefferson to John Adams, October 28, 1813, August 30, 1791, both in Cappon (ed.), *Adams-Jefferson Letters*, II, 391, I, 252; "In fact I do not feel an interest in any pencil but that of David," Jefferson to Madame de Brehan, March 14, 1789, in Boyd, Butterfield, and Bryan (eds.), *Papers*, XIV, 656 (see also Howard C. Rice, Jr., *Jefferson's Paris*, 34); Jefferson to John Jay, July 19, 1789, in Boyd, Butterfield, and Bryan (eds.), *Papers*, XV, 289.

Most telling of all in Jefferson's portrayal of the French revolutionary crowd is his description of their conduct and self-discipline. It is almost as if Jefferson had been able to look ahead one hundred years and prepare a rebuttal for the arguments Gustave LeBon would use in attacking the "collective mind" of the crowd. Especially in his letters to friends in America, Jefferson portrays the Paris crowds as responsible, as capable of making discreet and not impetuous decisions, and as reflecting a capacity for fairness. So confident is Jefferson of the overall virtues of these crowds that he does nothing to conceal the violence they do commit. In its candor, the following letter to Thomas Paine is typical of Jefferson:

> Yesterday Monsr. Foulon one of the late obnoxious ministry was brought here from the country, where he had been taken, as is said by his own tenants. He was hung by the crowd, his head severed, and his body dragged through the principal streets. In the night was brought also Monsr. Bertier de Chauvigny, Intendant of Paris. . . . He was massacred as soon as he arrived. I still hope that nothing will revive the tumults but the possession of these obnoxious characters, and probably the examples already made will teach them to keep out of the way.[32]

This kind of street justice did not cause Jefferson to change his belief in the basic bravery and integrity of the French revolutionary crowd. In most of the clashes he describes, the crowd is the underdog and is pitted against well-armed troops. When the crowd wins a battle, it is often with weapons as crude as stones, and unless trapped in a building, the troops they are fighting have little difficulty retreating to safety. Equally important, the crowd Jefferson describes rarely seems bent on gratuitous or random violence. The few bloody executions Jefferson writes about are almost always of cruel officials. In the Paris battles he comments upon, the crowd consistently takes its objectives as peaceably as it can. Jefferson describes the capture of the Hôtel des Invalides as occurring without any loss of life and observes that the siege of the Bastille became violent only after the crowd was fired upon.[33]

This view of the conduct of the Paris crowds also holds for

32. Jefferson to Thomas Paine, July 23, 1789, in Boyd, Butterfield, and Bryan (eds.), *Papers*, XV, 302.
33. Jefferson to John Jay, July 19, 1789, *ibid.*, 287–88.

Jefferson's account of less celebrated moments of the Revolution. Here he is especially successful in capturing how unselfish and honest the Paris crowds could be, how often they were governed by a sense of moral economy. Over and over, Jefferson shows their conduct to be what we would expect from an intelligent and dedicated individual operating by a carefully elaborated revolutionary code. On the question of food, for example, Jefferson notes that the crowds do not let their hunger get the best of them but, on seizing "a great store of corn," carry it to the corn market. And with regard to money, Jefferson describes an even greater "severity of honesty," telling of reports that, when bags of money were offered as bribes, they were "uniformly refused by the mob." In Jefferson's closely focused portrait, the French revolutionary crowd is even capable of punishing its own. "There have been many reports of instantaneous executions by the mob, on such of their own body as they caught in acts of theft or robbery. Some of these may perhaps be true," he writes John Jay. Whether literally true or not is beside the point—Jefferson has made such actions credible with his detailed picture of the men and women of the Paris crowds. We are inclined to take his account in the spirit he offers it, just as we are inclined to believe that he is relying on experience and not merely defending a political position when he concludes, "It is impossible to conceive a greater fermentation than has worked in Paris, nor do I believe that so great a fermentation ever produced so little injury in any other place. I have been thro' it daily, have observed the mobs with my own eyes in order to be satisfied of their objects."[34]

Twelve years later, Jefferson the president would offer the nation a less sanguine view of the crowds of the French Revolution. No longer would he refer to them in terms of fermentation (a slow, natural process as indigenous to France as the making of wine). In his first inaugural address, Jefferson would instead describe the street activity of the French Revolution as "the throes and convulsions of the ancient world" and as "the agonizing spasms of infuriated man seeking through

34. Ibid., 290; Jefferson to Diodati, August 3, 1789, in ibid., 325.

blood and slaughter his long-lost liberty." He also would observe that "it was not wonderful that the agitation of the billows should reach even this distant and peaceful shore" and "divide opinions as to measures of safety."[35] This is a shift in emphasis we would expect from a president anxious to unify the country and sensitive to fears about his radicalism. But it is important to bear in mind that Jefferson's "First Inaugural" does not signal a change in the criteria he used for judging the crowd. In this matter he and Adams remained consistent to the end. They never stopped believing that in the face of tyranny, crowds had a legitimate political role to play, nor did they ever doubt that a representative crowd—one that embodied the various classes of a nation—could act with discipline and restraint. Indeed, for Adams and Jefferson the long-range problem posed by the standards they employed for judging the crowd had little to do with the standards themselves. Rather, it lay in the fact that the revolutionary experience which led them to take the crowd so seriously in the first place was not an experience that could be passed on.

35. Thomas Jefferson, "First Inaugural Address," in Foner (ed.), *Basic Writings of Thomas Jefferson*, 333.

II

The Crowd in the Classic American Novel

In the summer of 1831, a member of one of the most prominent landholding families in upstate New York told Alexis de Tocqueville, "All classes joined together in the Revolution. Afterwards the strength of democracy was so paramount that no one attempted to struggle against it."[1] James Fenimore Cooper also believed in this unifying view of the Revolution, and he saw all departures from it as politically destructive.

How destructive becomes dramatically apparent when we turn to the last of Cooper's Littlepage novels, *The Redskins.* There, a crowd of farmers, dressed as Indians, attacks the estate of Hugh Littlepage and tries to seize control of the feudal-style leases he holds on their land. In their disguises, and in their desire to break bonds dating back to the time when the English colonial government, continuing the policy of the Dutch patroon system, made huge land grants to a few families, Cooper's Indians bear a striking resemblance to those revolutionary Indians who three-quarters of a century earlier defied English authority and dumped a shipload of tea in Boston harbor.

This resemblance was deliberately cultivated by the tenant farmers in New York State who from 1839 to 1848 carried on a fierce antirent war with the most important families in the Hudson Valley. They saw their struggle to gain ownership of their farms as both revolutionary and traditional, believing themselves victims of the same kind of tyranny that had led their forefathers to challenge the Stamp Act. "We will take up the ball of Revolution where our fathers stopped it and roll it to the final consummation of freedom and independence of

1. Staughton Lynd, *Class Conflict, Slavery, and the Constitution* (Indianapolis, 1967), 25.

the masses," they pledged in the July 4, 1839, declaration that announced the start of their movement.[2] For a New York landowner such as Cooper, no historical analogy could have been more repellent. He looked upon the "calico Indians" of the Hudson Valley as a threat to everything his family stood for, and he transferred these feelings to his writings. The tenant farmers in *The Redskins* are not portrayed as a nineteenth-century version of the revolutionary crowd that won the approval of John Adams and Thomas Jefferson. They are instead a crowd that by weight of numbers and political power represents a new form of tyranny in America.

This fear of a tyrannical majority in action had been festering in Cooper for over a decade. Although an admirer of Jefferson, a friend of Lafayette's, and a supporter of the Democratic party of Andrew Jackson, the Cooper who returned to America in 1833 after seven years in Europe was a man who found the egalitarian politics of his native country profoundly disturbing. In his political treatise *The American Democrat*, published just three years after *Democracy in America*, Cooper is, if anything, more worried than Tocqueville by the American tendency "to defer to the publick in opposition to truth and justice." But unlike Tocqueville, he will not qualify his observations by insisting that in America the tyranny of the majority "has had more effect on the mores than on the behavior of society."[3] The crowd that horrifies Cooper is a physical as well as a social force, and he describes it in terms of demagogues, violence, and above all, "the disgraceful desire to govern by means of mobs."[4]

The same perspective also dominates the two novels, *Homeward Bound* and *Home as Found*, that Cooper published at

2. Philip S. Foner (ed.), *We, the Other People* (Urbana, 1976), 60. See also Henry Christman, *Tin Horns and Calico* (New York, 1945).
3. See James Franklin Beard (ed.), *The Letters and Journals of James Fenimore Cooper* (6 vols.; Cambridge, Mass., 1968), I, 242–43, II, 7–8, 187–229 (Lafayette), I, 95–96, II, 31–33 (Jefferson), I, 402, VI, 323–24 (Jackson); James Fenimore Cooper, *The American Democrat* (New York, 1956), 145; Alexis de Tocqueville, *Democracy in America*, ed. J. P. Mayer (Garden City, 1969), 257. Tocqueville does not see the crowd as the means by which the tyranny of the majority manifests itself. When he does talk about crowds, it is in a footnote in which he speaks of "a rabble more dangerous even than that of European towns" (278).
4. Cooper, *The American Democrat*, 148.

this time. In them the Effingham family find that, on returning to America after a stay in Europe, they cannot, any more
than could the Coopers, live as before. They must defend the
very land they own against the "politico-pious" claims of an
"omnipotent, overruling, law-making, law-breaking public,"
and although the Effinghams prove their right to their land,
their victory leaves only bitterness between them and their
neighbors. In the end, they are left with the political vision
that John Effingham advances when he declares, "Excited
men, acting in masses, compose what are called mobs and
have committed a thousand excesses."[5]

By the middle 1840s, when he began his Littlepage trilogy,
Cooper was set for an all-out attack on an America ruled by a
body politic willing "to substitute popularity for the right."
His timing for venting his bitter feelings could not have been
better. The New York State rent wars were just entering their
final phase. The defiance that tenant mobs had shown to land-
lords, their agents, and sheriffs bent on seizing their property
was finally paying off with public sympathy, and in the Littlepage novels, Cooper created a fictional family that permitted
him to comment on the damage done when "the people themselves happen to go astray *en masse*."[6] Revolutionary officers
and landowners who settled their original tenants at great personal expense, the Littlepages are ideal patriots and gentry,
and in the first two novels of the trilogy, their authority reigns
supreme. The only serious challenge to their way of life comes
from a greedy squatter, Aaron Thousandacres, and he is finally routed. By 1846 and *The Redskins*, however, this harmony has disappeared. Hugh Littlepage must now defend the
Littlepage estate at Ravensnest against men who care only
about having their leases changed and who do not appreciate
the role his family has played in New York since before the
Revolution.

In Cooper's eyes, this was the kind of crowd that by the
1840s was able to "make the magistrates" and "elect the sheriffs," and he saw few limits to its power. The key fact about

5. James Fenimore Cooper, *Home as Found* (New York, 1896), 209, 205, 209.
6. *Ibid.*, 226; James Fenimore Cooper, *The Redskins* (New York, 1896),
424. On the politics of the Littlepage novels, see A. N. Kaul, *The American
Vision* (New Haven, 1964), 84–120.

the crowd that attacks Ravensnest is that it consists not of the poor but of men and women at the middle levels of society—respectable tenant farmers as well as an ambitious lawyer. Although an improbable alliance of real Indians and an incorruptible sheriff makes it possible for the Littlepages to defeat their attackers, *The Redskins* ends on a note that reflects the dramatic changes that would come to upstate New York by 1852, when a series of legislative and court decisions forced such landowners as the Van Rensselaers to break up their estates. Hugh Littlepage realizes that he can never have peace as a landlord, and on the Sunday after the attack on his home, he acknowledges the political hopelessness of his situation. "America no longer seemed America to my eyes," he remarks, "suddenly and painfully conscious of the character and extent of the combination" that has put him on the defensive. *The Redskins* closes with Hugh and his new wife leaving New York for Washington, D.C., and with the "editor" of the Littlepage manuscripts commenting that if Washington should fail him, Hugh still has Florence, Italy, "where he can reside among the other victims of oppression, with the advantage of being admired as a refugee from republican tyranny."[7]

For Cooper, the migration of the Littlepages marks the end of an era, but in terms of American fiction, the demise of the Littlepages signals a turning point of a far different sort. What it provides is a paradigm of how a classic American novelist who believed in the democratic values of the Revolution could by the mid-nineteenth century find a crowd composed of a representative majority of his fellow citizens a threat to national life.

That a classic American novelist should, a half century after the Revolution, come to look on the crowd in this fashion makes complete political sense. By the 1820s, the problem an expanding America faced was no longer one of independence but one of national union. As Daniel Webster reminded his listeners at the 1825 groundbreaking ceremony for the Bunker Hill Monument, they could "win no laurels in a war for independence." Their task was "the great duty of defence and pres-

7. Cooper, *The Redskins,* 391, 506.

ervation." It was up to them to "cultivate a true spirit of union." The majority crowd of the classic American novel now spoke to the issue of national unity and the cost of achieving it as well. But this time the consequences of the crowd's actions were vastly different. When the majority crowd of the classic American novel overstepped its bounds, its principal victims were individuals, often those least able to defend themselves, and what was undermined was the idea of America as a nation in which personal freedom was a vital part of the political fabric.[8]

The implications of this changed view of the crowd take on even greater weight when we turn to the work of Nathaniel Hawthorne, Herman Melville, and Mark Twain. In their most important novels, the majority crowd is specifically identified with the legal system, the nation's ongoing conquest of nature, and the struggle over slavery. In *The Scarlet Letter* it is a grim "crowd of Puritans" who turn Hester's punishment into a social drama. In *Moby Dick* it is the crew of the *Pequod*, unified and acting as a mob, who carry out Ahab's hunt for the White Whale. In *Huckleberry Finn* it is a "crowd" of fifteen armed farmers who pursue Jim when he escapes. But most significantly, what these fictional crowds have in common— what makes even Hawthorne's seventeenth-century Puritans a reflection of his generation—is their preoccupation with political conformity.[9]

We only begin to describe the shared profile these crowds have when we note that in background and class they represent most, if not all, of conventional society. Far more telling is that each of these crowds, despite its representative nature, does not act as though it were "the people." Its loyalty is to those in authority, and time and again it serves the needs of authority, whether institutional or personal. Nothing seems to animate the majority crowd of the classic American novel

8. Daniel Webster, "The Bunker Hill Monument," in Edwin P. Whipple (ed.), *The Great Speeches and Orations of Daniel Webster* (Boston, 1894), 135; Edward Pessen, *Jacksonian America* (Homewood, Ill., 1978), 33; Page Smith, *The Nation Comes of Age* (New York, 1981), xi–xii.
9. Nathaniel Hawthorne, *The Scarlet Letter* (Columbus, 1963), 56; Herman Melville, *Moby Dick* (Indianapolis, 1964), 701; Mark Twain, *Adventures of Huckleberry Finn*, ed. Walter Blair and Victor Fischer (Berkeley, 1985), 336.

more than the opportunity to level whomever or whatever is exceptional. At the height of its anger, we see it venting itself on a target—an adulterous woman, a white whale, a runaway slave—that is symbol of and scapegoat for a multitude of dissatisfactions.

The strain of seeing American political life in these terms is expressed in an observation Melville made to Hawthorne. "It seems an inconsistency to assert unconditional democracy in all things, and yet to confess a dislike to all mankind—in the mass. But not so," he wrote. What Melville's remark points up is that, as long as the American writer saw the majority crowd in the terms he did, he was forever wedded to a terrible paradox. The democratic values he believed in were in constant jeopardy from the collective actions of the very people on whom their preservation depended. In this context, there was leeway for Hawthorne, Melville, and Twain to explore the appeal of a life based on social escape or to find hope in the political middle ground embodied in the idea of fraternity.[10] But in their fiction these alternatives were not permanent solutions. In the end, the political question on which their novels turned was the question they insisted their principal characters live with throughout their lives: Could American democracy be anything more than the coercive mass democracy of the crowd?

In an 1855 letter to his publisher, Hawthorne observed, "America is now wholly given over to a d——d mob of scribbling women, and I should have no chance of success while the public is occupied with their trash."[11] For the most part, however, Hawthorne uses the words *crowd* and *mob* with much greater care. When we survey his work, we see the degree to which his understanding of American political life is inseparable from his sense of the crowd.

The House of the Seven Gables illustrates Hawthorne's awareness of the crowd's simultaneous appeal and danger. In

10. Melville to Nathaniel Hawthorne, June 1, 1851, in William H. Gilman (ed.), *The Letters of Herman Melville* (New Haven, 1965), 127. See also Wilson Carey McWilliams, *The Idea of Fraternity in America* (Berkeley, 1973), 301–402.

11. Hawthorne to William Ticknor, January, 1855, in Caroline Ticknor, *Hawthorne and His Publisher* (Boston, 1913), 141.

the chapter "The Arched Window," a simple political procession turns out to be anything but innocent when seen
from the perspective of the reclusive Clifford Pyncheon, who
is tempted to lose himself in "the rush and roar of the human
tide" passing below his balcony. Hawthorne's primary point is
that the crowd, by virtue of its "surging stream of human
sympathies," can be overwhelming for anyone who sees it
naïvely. From such a perspective, the crowd offers both the
power of a "mighty river of life" and collective safety, because
"it melts all the petty personalities of which it is made up,
into one broad mass of existence."[12]

Hawthorne's awareness of the crowd's sirenlike potential
did not, however, put him in blind opposition to it. On questions of class, his democratic instincts ran deep enough for
him to observe in his *Italian Notebooks* of 1858, "I remember
in America, I had an innate antipathy to constables, and always sided with the mob against law." He also knew the vital
role the crowd had played in the American Revolution. In
1840 he wrote of the sacking of the house of Lieutenant Governor Thomas Hutchinson, "That was a moment when a loyalist and aristocrat, like Hutchinson, might have learnt how
powerless are kings, nobles, and great men when the low and
humble range themselves against them."[13]

In Hawthorne's judgment, the real danger posed by the
crowd, especially the majority crowd, came from the fact that,
time and again in the name of values it held sacred, it sought
to impose an artificial unity on society. Those who composed
such dangerous crowds did not themselves have to be evil.
Like the mob of reformers in "Earth's Holocaust," who in
their zeal burn books, a crowd could be a menace when convinced it was improving the world. This was the kind of political tyranny Hawthorne most feared. In the campaign biography he undertook of Franklin Pierce, his friend and Bowdoin
College classmate, Hawthorne praised Pierce for his "unob-
trusive" legislative career and for his opposition to the cen-
tralizing trends of the times. There is a direct parallel between

12. Nathaniel Hawthorne, *The House of the Seven Gables* (Columbus,
1965), 165.
13. Nathaniel Hawthorne, *The French and Italian Notebooks* (Columbus,
1980), 330; Nathaniel Hawthorne, "Liberty Tree," in *True Stories* (Columbus,
1972), 157.

the Hawthorne who at the peak of his literary career gives so much attention to the oppressive crowd of *The Scarlet Letter*, and the Hawthorne who in his *Life of Franklin Pierce* writes that Andrew Jackson's veto of the Maysville Road Bill saved America from a system that would have placed "the capital of our federative Union in a position resembling imperial Rome, where once each independent state was a subject province, and all the highways of the world were said to meet in her forum." Crowds that prompted the kind of America that Jackson in his "Farewell Address" described as a nation in which prosperity and happiness do not come "at the expense of others" were crowds Hawthorne approved of. Those that promoted political unity at the cost of "individual freedom" were crowds he saw as threatening.[14]

The outlines of this approach to the crowd emerge with particular clarity in the account of the American Revolution that Hawthorne wrote for children, *The Whole History of Grandfather's Chair*. There, Hawthorne sets himself apart from "other historians" by minimizing the importance of military battles and focusing on a series of street encounters between British rulers and American mobs. The encounters do not always shed glory on the patriot cause, but the point Hawthorne returns to again and again is their necessity. "It is probable that the petitions of Congress would have had little or no effect on the British statesmen," he observes, "if the violent deeds of the American people had not shown how much excited the people were."[15]

The same distinctions carry over to Hawthorne's fictional accounts of the Revolution. They are dominated by the values of a man who described himself as a "thorough-going democrat" and believed that in America, democracy was "a natural growth" that occurred "in simplicity, as if there were no other way for people to be ruled." In "The Gray Champion," Hawthorne describes the Boston Massacre as an encounter between "the troops of Britain" and "a people struggling against

14. Nathaniel Hawthorne, *Life of Franklin Pierce* (Boston, 1883), 371, 369; Andrew Jackson, "Farewell Address," in James D. Richardson (ed.), *Messages and Papers of the Presidents* (11 vols.; New York, 1907), III, 298; James R. Mellow, *Nathaniel Hawthorne in His Times* (Boston, 1980), 534.
15. Hawthorne, "Liberty Tree," in *True Stories*, 184, 152.

her tyranny." In the stories that comprise his "Legends of the Province House," he is no less unequivocal in characterizing the revolutionary crowd as a defender of liberty. In "Edward Randolph's Portrait," the gentle Alice Vane insists, "When the rulers feel themselves irresponsible, it were well that they should be reminded of the awful weight of a People's curse." By contrast, her uncle, Lieutenant Governor Thomas Hutchinson, rationalizes his harsh policies by equating the crowd with the lower orders of American society rather than with the population as a whole. "What to me is the outcry of a mob, in this remote province of the realm?" he asks. "The King is my master, and England is my country! Upheld by their armed strength, I set foot upon the rabble, and defy them." [16]

What makes Hawthorne's analysis of the revolutionary crowd so fascinating—and so consistent with his later fiction—is that the thorough-going democrat in him never gets the best of the political skeptic. In *Grandfather's Chair*, Hawthorne's narrator is quick to express sympathy for the rough treatment accorded the aging Loyalist, Andrew Oliver, and to admit that a patriot mob's attack on the personal property of a British official is "most unjustifiable." [17] In his fiction, Hawthorne is equally evenhanded. The positive picture that he offers of the revolutionary crowd in "The Gray Champion" and "Legends of the Province House" must be weighed against the very different and more detailed view in "My Kinsman, Major Molineux."

This contrast is apparent in the opening paragraph of "My Kinsman, Major Molineux," in which Hawthorne notes that the colonists' self-interest rather than political principle was often the reason for revolutionary activity. "The people looked with most jealous scrutiny to the exercise of power which did not emanate from themselves," he writes, "and they usually repaid their rulers with slender gratitude for the compliances

16. Hawthorne's description of himself occurs in "Old Esther Dudley," in *Twice-Told Tales* (Columbus, 1974), 291. In "Grandfather's Chair" we find a highly sympathetic account of the growth of democracy in the colonies (*True Stories*, 33). Nathaniel Hawthorne, "The Gray Champion," in *Twice-Told Tales*, 10; Nathaniel Hawthorne, "Edward Randolph's Portrait," in *Twice-Told Tales*, 262, 266.

17. Hawthorne, "Old Esther Dudley," in *Twice-Told Tales*, 291; Hawthorne, "Liberty Tree," in *True Stories*, 159.

by which, in softening their instructions from beyond the sea, they had incurred the reprehension of those who gave them."[18]

Hawthorne is leading to the point that revolutionary action can be justified only when it is inseparable from genuine political liberation, and this belief colors the rest of his story. As Robin Molineux searches for his kindly loyalist uncle, Major Molineux, the colonists he meets do not represent an America on the verge of political uniqueness so much as a country flawed by what Hawthorne in "The Gray Champion" called "all those abominations which had driven the Puritans to the wilderness." The men and women Robin encounters know that his uncle is about to be the victim of an uprising, and they treat Robin's naïve inquiries with brutal mockery. Everywhere Robin goes, he is greeted with laughter, and the laughter leads directly to the climax of the story, in which the major is tarred and feathered in a scene of frenzied merriment. What happens at this point, however, exceeds in its violence the cruelty that came before, and shows that, gathered together in a crowd, Robin's tormentors are capable of far greater cruelty than as individuals.[19]

Shouts and laughter draw Robin to the scene of his uncle's humiliation, and it is through Robin's eyes that the reader sees the "scattered individuals" of the town transform themselves into a mob:

> A mighty stream of people now emptied into the street, and came rolling slowly towards the church. A single horseman wheeled the corner in the midst of them . . . the red of one cheek was an emblem of fire and sword; the blackness of the other betokened the mourning that attends them. In his train were wild figures in the Indian dress, and many fantastic shapes without a model, giving the whole march a visionary air, as if a dream had broken forth from some feverish brain, and were sweeping visibly through the midnight streets.

It is a moment of bewildering excitement for Robin, but Hawthorne will not let us forget that what is going on is controlled

18. Nathaniel Hawthorne, "My Kinsman, Major Molineux," in *The Snow Image and Uncollected Tales* (Columbus, 1974), 208.
19. Hawthorne, "The Gray Champion," in *Twice-Told Tales*, 13; Hawthorne, "My Kinsman, Major Molineux," in *The Snow Image*, 230.

political violence. When those in charge of the crowd want order, they get it immediately. "A moment more and the leader thundered a command to halt; the trumpets vomited a horrid breath, and then held their peace; the shouts and laughter of the people died away, and there remained only a universal hum, allied to silence."[20]

What follows is Robin's moral undoing. He sides with "the people" not out of political conviction, as Alice Vane does, but because the crowd frightens him into conforming. The "unexpected appearance of the crowd, the torches, the confused din" affect Robin with a "mental inebriety," and as the "contagion" of the crowd's laughter spreads, Robin too becomes infected. He cannot escape the disease of the crowd. The pity and terror he felt on first seeing his uncle give way to a laughter louder than anyone else's. Instead of remaining loyal to his uncle, Robin sides with the crowd. It is not, however, Robin's fall that brings "My Kinsman, Major Molineux" to its conclusion, but as Hawthorne's contagion metaphor implies, the analogy between Robin and America coming of age. Both are worse off than they know, victims of a crowd that in the name of a new political order is as tyrannical as any old-world regime.[21]

An even greater sense of the relationship between the crowd and America's origins dominates *The Scarlet Letter*, but with Hawthorne's masterpiece it is essential not only to look back to seventeenth-century New England but to remember that the majority crowd which oppresses Hester is, by Hawthorne's Jacksonian lights, a modern crowd as well. In its insistence on conformity, this crowd duplicates the political order he saw in his own lifetime as "so dangerous to liberty and to public and private integrity."[22]

The seriousness with which Hawthorne took the crowd of

20. Hawthorne, "My Kinsman, Major Molineux," in *The Snow Image*, 227, 299, 228.

21. *Ibid.*, 227, 299. See also Q. D. Leavis, "Hawthorne as Poet," in Charles Feidelson, Jr., and Paul Brodtkorb (eds.), *Interpretations of American Literature* (New York, 1959), 48. She describes Major Molineux being driven from town with the "rough music" that in old England was used to drive undesirables from the community.

22. Hawthorne, *Life of Franklin Pierce*, 369.

The Scarlet Letter is apparent immediately. The crowd is present from the start and characterized in detail in the novel's opening paragraph:

> The grass-plot before the jail, in Prison Lane, on a certain summer morning, not less than two centuries ago, was occupied by a pretty large number of the inhabitants of Boston; all with their eyes intently fastened on the iron-clamped oaken door. Amongst any other population, or at a later period in the history of New England, the grim physiognomies of these good people would have augured some awful business in hand. . . . But, in the early severity of the Puritan character, an inference of this kind could not so indubitably be drawn . . . from a people amongst whom religion and law were almost identical, and in whose character both were so thoroughly interfused, that the mildest and the severest acts of public discipline were alike made venerable and awful.

As soon as Hester Prynne steps out of prison branded as an adulteress, she must deal with this avenging "throng of bearded men, in sad-colored garments and gray, steeple-crowned hats, intermixed with women, some wearing hoods, and others bare-headed."[23]

This confrontation is filled with historical import for Hawthorne, who explicitly identifies Hester's plight with that of "the sainted Ann Hutchinson." When we turn to his biographical sketch "Mrs. Hutchinson," we see details that appear there also appear in *The Scarlet Letter*. At her antinomian trial, Ann Hutchinson also faces "a crowd of hooded women, and of men in steeple-hats," and as she stands loftily before her judges, Hawthorne comments that her fate is to be decided in a context where "religious freedom was wholly inconsistent with public safety." The latter point cannot be emphasized too strongly. A man who believed that government should "grow out of the nature of things and the character of the people," Hawthorne never objected to rulers taking political precautions. He concedes that need in the first chapter of *The Scarlet Letter*, where he writes that the founders of a new colony, "whatever Utopia of human virtue and happiness they might originally project," have invariably deemed it necessary "to allot a portion as the site of a prison." What troubles

23. Hawthorne, *The Scarlet Letter*, 49, 47.

Hawthorne is the authoritarian nature of the social control the Puritans attempt to exercise.[24]

It is the Puritans' excessive response to an offense that was, as Edmund Morgan notes in his essay, "The Puritans and Sex," relatively frequent in seventeenth-century New England that makes for Hawthorne's drama and gives the Puritan crowd, not simply Puritan society, such importance.[25] Were Hawthorne a Dickens describing an ancient and corrupt legal system, then a trial scene followed by extensive social criticism would accomplish his purposes. But Hawthorne is not content to offer old-world criticisms of new-world justice. His target is the politicization—the obscenely democratic nature—of Hester's punishment and the way the Puritan magistrates use the crowd to reinforce their power.

It is this brutalizing political process that makes the crowd so crucial in *The Scarlet Letter* and the images of rigidity Hawthorne uses to characterize it so telling. The Puritan leaders are men such that "out of the whole human family, it would not have been easy to select the same number of wise and virtuous persons, who should be less capable of sitting in judgment on an erring woman's heart." But they are able to exercise their judgment in this dictatorial way because it is enforced by a crowd willing to do their bidding. "The witnesses of Hester Prynne's disgrace," Hawthorne observes, "were stern enough to look upon her death, had that been the sentence, without a murmur at its severity." Hawthorne remarks that "a Papist among the crowd of Puritans" might have seen in Hester and Pearl "the image of Divine Maternity," but this view is his alone. When those in the crowd speak, they do so, with the exception of a young wife holding a child by the hand, to agree with their leaders or to call for even harsher penalties against Hester. The women in the crowd are especially cruel in this regard. One wants to have Hester marked with a branding iron. Another calls for her death, declaring,

24. *Ibid.*, 148; Nathaniel Hawthorne, "Mrs. Hutchinson," in *Tales, Sketches and Other Papers* (Boston, 1883), 220, 224, 222; Hawthorne, "The Gray Champion," in *Twice-Told Tales*, 13; Hawthorne, *The Scarlet Letter*, 47.
25. Edmund Morgan, "The Puritans and Sex," in Michael Gordon (ed.), *The American Family in Social-Historical Perspective* (New York, 1973), 285–86.

"This woman has brought shame upon us all, and ought to die. Is there not a law for it?"[26]

For Hester, what follows from her treatment by the crowd is seven years of aloneness. She is forced into an isolation that neither ordinary society nor mere imprisonment could have caused, and during the next seven years her moments of relief are few. On the night of John Winthrop's death when she, Dimmesdale, and Pearl stand alone on the pillory, Hester does feel some hope, and eventually "individuals in private life" come to look on the scarlet letter as a token of Hester's many good deeds. But as we see in the chapter "The Procession," the Puritans' original view of Hester is never completely put aside. When at the end of *The Scarlet Letter* the town comes together on election day and people move about as a crowd rather than as individuals, earlier feelings toward Hester are revived. As in "My Kinsman, Major Molineux," the result is an ending in which personal and political tragedy are inseparable. We are left with a new-world community that has sought to impose a collective virtue on itself and instead achieved a repressive solidarity lacking the most elementary Christian values.[27]

The political order achieved by the crowd turns out to be the opposite of that advocated by John Winthrop on the flagship *Arbella*, when he proposed founding a community whose members would "entertain each other in brotherly affection" and be "knit together." Only Hester and the sorority of women who gather at her cottage come close to such a model of Christian charity. But to see Hester as a political prophetess— even an intermediary one, as Sacvan Bercovitch argues in *The Puritan Origins of the American Self*—is to turn away from the darker implications of Hawthorne's story.[28] The failure of the crowd to counterbalance the Puritan magistrates and Puritan law leads to a political conclusion untempered by Hawthorne's celebrated ambiguity. His conclusion reveals an America in which there is no powerful democratic force the weak can appeal to, and it suggests that the people (as Haw-

26. Hawthorne, *The Scarlet Letter*, 64, 56.
27. *Ibid.*, 162, 246.
28. John Winthrop, "A Model of Christian Charity," in Perry Miller (ed.), *The American Puritans* (Garden City, 1956), 83; Sacvan Bercovitch, *The Puritan Origins of the American Self* (New Haven, 1975), 177.

thorne uses that term) have the collective potential to be their own worst enemy.

The people in *The Scarlet Letter* show their "benign countenance" only when they remain apart. But as Hawthorne realized, in an expanding America, intent on becoming a single nation, the people were bound to find more and more occasions for banding together. Power, as Abraham Lincoln shrewdly observed, would increasingly go to "whoever molds public sentiment." The crowd of *The Scarlet Letter* not only anticipates the post-revolutionary mob of *Dr. Grimshawe's Secret*, which makes the doctor a target simply because he remains aloof. It also leads us beyond Hawthorne's fiction to his much neglected 1862 *Atlantic Monthly* essay, "Chiefly About War Matters." There, to the consternation of his *Atlantic* editors, Hawthorne showed himself to be anything but a staunch northern patriot. Unlike Emerson, Hawthorne has no faith that the war "breaks through all that is not real as itself." He patronizes Lincoln. He asserts that John Brown was "justly hanged." And he predicts that freedom will prove of little benefit to the present generation of former slaves. But what lies at the core of Hawthorne's essay is his belief that "no human effort, on a grand scale, has ever resulted according to the purpose of its projectors. The advantages are always incidental." Hawthorne might well have leveled this criticism against the Puritan crowd of *The Scarlet Letter*, and the fact that he might have reminds us once again of how deeply intertwined Hawthorne's sense of history and the crowd were. A decade after the publication of *The Scarlet Letter*, the coercive unity that Hester's oppressors seek parallels nothing so much as the "unnatural" desire for union that Hawthorne—no friend of abolitionism—saw destroying the country.[29]

Like Hawthorne, Herman Melville also saw the majority crowd as a growing danger for America. To understand the his-

29. Hawthorne, *The Scarlet Letter*, 162; Abraham Lincoln, "Notes for Speeches," in John G. Nicolay and John Hay (eds.), *Complete Works of Abraham Lincoln* (12 vols.; New York, 1905), IV, 222; Joel Porte (ed.), *Emerson in His Journals* (Cambridge, Mass., 1982), 506; Nathaniel Hawthorne, "Chiefly About War Matters," in *Tales, Sketches, and Other Papers*, 310–13, 327, 319, 332; Mellow, *Nathaniel Hawthorne in His Times*, 536. See also George M. Fredrickson, *The Inner Civil War* (New York, 1965), 1–4.

torical context in which Melville's description of the crowd occurs in *Moby Dick*, the best starting point is a speech, "The Constitution and the Union," which Daniel Webster delivered in the Senate twenty-five years after his Bunker Hill Monument address. In "The Constitution and the Union," Webster's mind is still on the relationship between contemporary America and the America of the Founding Fathers, but now the whole tenor of his concern is different. The country is, he fears, about to come apart, and in supporting the Compromise of 1850 as a political remedy, he is at pains to make his own steadfastness clear. "I am looking out for no fragment upon which to float away from the wreck, if wreck there must be," he declares. "I speak to-day for the preservation of the Union."[30]

The sense of crisis that radiates from Webster's prose in "The Constitution and the Union" was something Melville felt as well, and in *Moby Dick* he focused on the majority crowd in a way that capitalized on these feelings. Certainly it is no accident that in his masterpiece, Melville chose to liken America to a ship. In doing so he was, as Alan Heimert has pointed out in his essay, "*Moby Dick* and American Political Symbolism," using figurative language his readers were familiar with. At mid century, references to the American ship of state were to be found everywhere. They were part of the Senate's vocabulary, as well as Lincoln's speeches, Longfellow's poetry, and Theodore Parker's essays.[31]

In *Moby Dick*, the metaphor of America as a ship of state allowed Melville to portray the country as a political creation needing to be held together, rather than as one that could be defined as timeless. On the basis of this idea, he could equate the *Pequod*'s thirty-man crew, "federated along one keel," with the thirty states in the Union. And he could picture the majority crowd, as represented by the crew after Ahab whips

30. Daniel Webster, "The Constitution and the Union," in Whipple (ed.), *The Great Speeches of Daniel Webster*, 601.
31. See Abraham Lincoln, "Reply to the Presbyterian General Assembly," in Nicolay and Hay (eds.), *Complete Works*, VIII, 288; Henry Wadsworth Longfellow, "The Building of the Ship"; Theodore R. Parker, "The Political Destination of America and the Signs of the Times," quoted in Alan Heimert, "*Moby Dick* and American Political Symbolism," *American Quarterly*, XV (Fall, 1963), 499.

them into a moblike fury, as the most powerful and dangerous
force for national unity, one capable of making a reality of
Webster's fears.[32]

Melville's indictment of the majority crowd, however, begins like Hawthorne's, with sympathy for the revolutionary
crowd. Melville was aware that there were political circumstances in which the revolutionary crowd was absolutely necessary, and in *Moby Dick* he makes the case for it in "The
Town-Ho's Story." There he offers the tale of an insurrection
similar to those occurring in France during the Revolution of
1848. The result is a chapter with many twists but a clear political outcome. A mutiny led by Steelkit, a sailor from "the
heart of our America," against Radney, the *Town-Ho*'s cruel
mate and part owner, is justified by Melville in principle and
along the class lines it takes. The tyranny Radney stands for is
seen as insufferable, and he is killed in pursuit of Moby Dick.
Steelkit and his supporters, on the other hand, behave in ad-
mirable, democratic fashion. Entrenching themselves behind
a barricade like "sea Parisians," they keep bloodshed to a
minimum and after a long struggle win their freedom.[33]

The crew of the *Pequod* find enough relevance in the *Town-
Ho*'s story to keep it secret from their officers, and throughout
Moby Dick, Melville heightens the crew's secrecy by hinting
at the possibility of a mutiny. After he tells them of his plans
to hunt Moby Dick, Ahab worries that his crew might "refuse
all further obedience to him," and at one point his conduct
does elicit "a half mutinous cry." But there is no one with
Steelkit's force of personality and democratic instincts aboard
the *Pequod*. Starbuck, the one officer who might lead a rebellion, objects to his captain's conduct on purely utilitarian
grounds, insisting that he remain loyal to the ship's owners
and "the way of business we follow."[34] As a result, Ahab and
not Starbuck ends up in control of the *Pequod*, and in so doing
makes the majority crowd rather than the revolutionary crowd
the central political issue.

In *Subversive Genealogy: The Politics and Art of Herman
Melville*, Michael Rogin asserts, "There is no realistic society

32. Melville, *Moby Dick*, 166.
33. *Ibid.*, 324, 333.
34. *Ibid.*, 286, 644, 220.

on the *Pequod* made coherent by relations among its characters. The *Pequod* is unified symbolically by the hunt for the
white whale." It is an ingenious argument, one that later leads
Rogin to conclude that in his pursuit of nature's leviathan,
Ahab creates the "artificial man" Hobbes equates with the
state in his *Leviathan*. What Rogin's argument omits, however, is the step that makes the hunt possible in the first
place—Ahab's conversion of his crew into a moblike unit
driven to attack Moby Dick. This transformation, achieved in
a setting in which there is not, as there is in *The Scarlet
Letter*, a genteel deference to authority, defines Ahab's political genius and links the politics of *Moby Dick* to an America
in which the crew (the thirty states) is described as *"Isolatoes"* and whaling, as Charles Olson long ago pointed out, is
the classic American enterprise, a blend of the hunt and hard
labor, the frontier and industry.[35]

The best way to trace the metamorphosis of the *Pequod*'s
crew into a moblike unit willing to hunt Moby Dick is to begin with the power Ahab exercises as a business and political
figure. Harry Levin argues that "Ahab can be historically
placed among those captains of industry and freebooters of
enterprise who, at the public expense, were so rapidly transforming the age." The truth of the matter is less grandiose and
more telling. Ahab is not a capitalist owner but a business figure with a different role to play, that of manager. His power
resides in his ability to control the men below him and reflects an economy in which more and more authority was
shifting to middlemen.[36]

The political significance of Ahab's managerial role is caught
perfectly by Harry B. Henderson in *Versions of the Past* in
which he contends, "The relations of Ahab and his crew rather
exemplify a perverse form of democratic centralism than an
outright despotism. The crew is not only 'commanded' by
Ahab, but is wooed and won to his purpose as he converts his

35. Michael Paul Rogin, *Subversive Genealogy: The Politics and Art of
Herman Melville* (New York, 1983), 107, 140; Melville, *Moby Dick*, 166;
Charles Olson, *Call Me Ishmael* (New York, 1958), 23–25.
36. Harry Levin, *The Power of Blackness* (New York, 1960), 212. For a discussion of how the industrial revolution led to a split between entrepreneurs
and managers, see Sidney Pollard, *The Genesis of Modern Management*
(Cambridge, Mass., 1965), 1–24, 104–59, 250–72.

formal authority into a nightmare version of a Jacksonian democratic dictatorship." This specific analogy is one that Melville encourages first by speaking of Jackson as a man God picked up from the "kingly commons" and "thundered higher than a throne" and then by speaking of Ahab in the same majestic-democratic terms. What makes the analogy so mean- ingful for *Moby Dick* is the royal fashion in which Ahab is able to exact "homage" from crewmen whose worth has been objectified from the moment they signed on and agreed to be paid in "lays," shares based on the *Pequod*'s owners' judgment of their labor value.[37]

In this context, Melville's allusion to Andrew Jackson stresses the fact that in the America he was describing, any- one after absolute political power could achieve it only by get- ting a majority of the electorate behind him. In contrast to Hawthorne's Jefferson-like Jackson, Melville's Ahab-like Jack- son is the president labeled "King Andrew" by his political opponents. He is the kind of spellbinding orator we see in George Caleb Bingham's *Stump Speaking*, and his audience, like the motley crowds that fill the Election Series paintings Bingham did in the 1850s, includes all ranks of society.[38] As a political King Andrew, Ahab is not, however, interested in being the servant of the people. His aim is to bring his audi- ence around to his way of thinking. He wants to use their en- ergy and strength to achieve his undemocratic ends.

Ahab begins the process of gaining sovereignty over his crew and uniting them in the service of his obsession in "The Quarter Deck" chapter when he calls the "entire ship's com- pany together." Before the "not wholly unapprehensive faces" of his officers and seamen he begins to pace. Suddenly he pauses and cries, "What do you do when ye see a whale, men?" The "impulsive rejoinder" from "a score of clubbed voices" is "Sing out for him!" From this moment on, Ahab has his crew locked "within the Leyden jar of his own magnetic life." Like a politician who knows the feelings of his audience, he asks questions that always yield a chorus of right answers. His men

37. Harry B. Henderson, *Versions of the Past* (New York, 1974), 136; Melville, *Moby Dick*, 161, 198–99, 114.
38. See Albert Christ-Janer, *George Caleb Bingham: Frontier Painter of Missouri* (New York, 1975), 48–69.

realize what is happening but offer no resistance. "More and more strangely and fiercely glad and approving grew the countenance of the old man at every shout; while the mariners began to gaze curiously at each other, as if marvelling how it was they themselves became so excited at such seemingly purposeless questions."[39]

Ahab does not, however, rely on rhetoric alone to arouse his crew. He is too aware of the economic realities of the *Pequod* for that. He knows that there is a "community of interest" aboard ship based on the fact that the value of the lays the men have been promised depends on how much whale oil they bring back, and he builds on this desire for profit. As soon as he has his crew under his spell, Ahab produces a gold doubloon and nails it to the mast. The doubloon, he promises, will go to the first man who sights Moby Dick. The sailors' reaction is one of instant approval, and with their shouts of "Huzza! Huzza!" Ahab's quest and their cupidity are joined. They are no longer the same "*Isolatoes*" they once were, but have taken the first step toward becoming what Ishmael in "The Try Works" chapter will call the "material counterpart of their monomaniac commander's soul."[40]

At this point in the voyage, Ahab controls the wildness of the crew, and the men are described by Ishmael in terms of animal imagery that foreshadow their deaths:

> Turning to the harpooners, he [Ahab] ordered them to produce their weapons. Then ranging them before him near the capstan, with their harpoons in their hands, while his three mates stood at his side with their lances, and the rest of the ship's company formed a circle round the group; he stood for an instant searchingly eyeing every man of his crew. But those wild eyes met his, as the bloodshot eyes of the prairie wolves meet the eye of their leader, ere he rushes on at their head in the trail of the bison; but, alas only to fall into the hidden snare of the Indian.

At Ahab's command, every man on ship agrees to "hunt Moby Dick to his death," and the scene ends with "the frantic crew" shouting "cries and maledictions against the white whale." The difference between the crew now and earlier is unmis-

39. Melville, *Moby Dick*, 216, 217, 224, 217.
40. *Ibid.*, 197, 218, 166, 540.

takable. They can no longer be compared to the crowd in George Caleb Bingham's Election Series. In their capacity for violence, their choice of a scapegoat, and their acceptance of authoritarian leadership, they are much closer to the anti-abolitionist mobs Leonard Richards describes in "*Gentlemen of Property and Standing.*"[41]

For Ahab, rousing his crew has not been as difficult a task as he imagined, and in the next chapter, he analyzes what he has done. He admits that he has maneuvered his crew like pieces of machinery, using his fiery personality to set them off. "Twas not so hard a task. I thought to find one stubborn, at least," Ahab admits, "but my one cogged circle fits into all their various wheels, and they revolve. Or, if you will, like so many ant-hills of powder, they all stand before me; and I their match." This confession does not trouble Ahab's conscience. Like Jackson, who described his enemies as "monsters" and believed in the Union "at all hazards and at any price," Ahab will not compromise. He closes his soliloquy by using the language of industry conquering nature to define his "sultanism of the brain." "The path to my fixed purpose is laid with iron rails whereon my soul is grooved to run," he declares. "Over unsounded gorges, through the rifled hearts of mountains, under torrents' beds, unerringly I rush!"[42]

The one problem for Ahab in all of this is that his sudden mastery of his crew is not enough. He must keep them primed for the final assault on Moby Dick. He knows that the effect of his rhetoric cannot last, and that without the prospect of a profitable voyage, his crew will turn against him. "The permanent constitutional condition of the manufactured man, thought Ahab, is sordidness. . . . They may scorn cash now; but let some months go by, and no perspective promise of it to them, and then this same cash would soon cashier Ahab." To keep control over his men, Ahab continues "true to the natural, nominal purpose of the *Pequod*'s voyage."[43] He makes sure

---

41. *Ibid.*, 223, 225; Leonard L. Richards, "*Gentlemen of Property and Standing*": *Anti-Abolition Mobs in Jacksonian America* (New York, 1970), 129–42, 154–55.

42. Melville, *Moby Dick*, 226–27; John Bassett (ed.), *The Correspondence of Andrew Jackson* (7 vols.; Washington, D.C., 1935), IV, 502, 495.

43. Melville, *Moby Dick*, 285–86.

that his crew carry out their regular duties and never lose sight of the rewards that await them for a successful hunt.

The strategy works so well that only once does Ahab have to remind his men, "All your oaths to hunt the White Whale are as binding as mine." By the time the *Pequod* makes contact with Moby Dick, the ship is brimming with oil. The morale of the crew is so high that when the White Whale is sighted, "the men on the deck rushed to the rigging to behold the famous whale they had so long been pursuing." All Ahab has to do is rekindle the mob spirit he ignited earlier and be sure that the fever pitch of his crew makes them more rather than less efficient in carrying out their duties. Ahab gives his energy to this task, and in turn the crowd scenes at the conclusion of *Moby Dick* are a direct extension of those that took place earlier. Even the imagery of the previous chapters reappears. The "iron rails" metaphor that Ahab used to describe his soul's path is completed as Moby Dick is compared to "the mighty iron Leviathan of the modern railway," and the gold that Ahab offered to the first man to sight Moby Dick is again used as an incentive. Having himself claimed the gold for sighting Moby Dick before anyone else, Ahab now declares, "Whosoever of ye first raises him upon the day he shall be killed, this gold is that man's; and if on that day I shall again raise him, then, ten times its sum shall be divided among all of ye!"[44]

After a day of chasing Moby Dick, the spirit the men had showed comes back like "old wine worked anew," and whatever doubts they have are put aside. Starbuck's abortive resistance to Ahab's authority, the subtle differences in attitude among the crew, and the sailors' unarticulated feelings about Moby Dick are consumed by the galvanizing mob politics of the moment. With a new and binding twist, the bison imagery of "The Quarter-Deck" chapter returns. The men's fears are "routed, as timid prairie hares that scatter before the bounding bison," and once again, they come together with the unity and "headlong eagerness" Ahab wants.

> Whatever pale fears and forebodings some of them might have felt before; these were not only kept out of sight through the growing

44. *Ibid.*, 644, 688, 227, 699, 698.

awe of Ahab, but they were broken up, and on all sides routed, as timid prairie hares that scatter before the bounding bison. . . .
  They were one man, not thirty. For as one ship that held them through all; though it was put together of all contrasting things— oak, and maple, and pine wood; iron, and pitch, and hemp—yet all these ran into each other in the one concrete hull . . . so, all the individualities of the crew, this man's valor, that man's fear, guilt and guiltiness, all varieties were welded into oneness, and were all directed to that fatal goal which Ahab their one Lord and keel did point to.[45]

What follows is not chaos, however, but a classic example of what can happen when a previously disunited group of men becomes animated by a mob spirit and guided by an overriding sense of purpose. In its mob heroism, the ship's company responds to Ahab's urgings with an intensity that goes beyond anything it owes him or anything Bildad and Peleg, the absentee owners of the *Pequod*, might wish. Ahab, in turn, is wise enough to keep the pressure on his crew. He knows the days of deferential democracy are over, and like a good Jacksonian he never asks his men to follow him because he is "the right sort." To the end, his rhetoric is designed to fire the imagination of the average crewman aboard the *Pequod*.[46]

On each day of the final chase of Moby Dick, enough occurs to give the crew grounds for mutiny. But they never come close to rebelling. The separateness and lack of power the men knew as "*Isolatoes*" are no longer democratic safeguards but a void that Ahab exploits, the reason why his siren call for unity is so politically and psychologically appealing. Even if it costs them their lives, the crew of the *Pequod* will not return to the barren aloneness of their earlier egalitarian state. They have become totally absorbed in the ship, merging their identities with it. "The rigging lived. The mast-heads, like the tops of tall palms, were outspreadingly tufted with arms and legs."[47]

Ishmael, buoyed up by Queequeg's coffin, manages to survive the pursuit of Moby Dick, and by his survival to suggest

45. *Ibid.*, 700–701.
46. For a discussion of political rhetoric and the common man in antebellum America, see Douglas T. Miller, *The Birth of Modern America, 1820–1850* (Indianapolis, 1970), 155–56.
47. Melville, *Moby Dick*, 701.

that the bonds achieved by him and Queequeg are an answer
to the mob unity Ahab brings about. Yet, appealing as such an
interpretation of *Moby Dick* is, especially when put in the
communitarian framework Wilson Carey McWilliams offers
in *The Idea of Fraternity in America*, in the end it falls short.
It overlooks the harsh fact that, measured by the cost in human lives, the fraternity achieved by Ishmael and Queequeg is
overshadowed by the destruction of the *Pequod* by the whale.
Wreck imagery, analogous to that of Webster's speech "The
Constitution and the Union," dominates Melville's final pages.
When Ahab identifies the wood of the *Pequod*—oak, maple,
and pine—with the country, he is declaring what has been implicit throughout *Moby Dick*. The diverse nature of America
and its peculiarly isolated brand of democracy have allowed
him as captain to overcome "all the individualities of the
crew" and to turn them into a moblike unit devoted to his
purposes.[48]

For Melville, who had begun *Moby Dick* in Whitmanesque
fashion, celebrating "the arm that wields a pick or drives a
spike," this view of mass politics and the crowd was disillu-
sioning and made all the more painful by the fact that in the
1850s the violent and expansionist version of Jacksonianism
it represented was proving increasingly ruinous for America.[49]
Melville was not, however, willing to soften or to back away
from the political implications of *Moby Dick* in his later
work. From 1852 on, the destructive qualities he attributed to
the majority crowd in *Moby Dick* would be attributed by him
to all crowds.

During the Civil War years, Whitman would take every opportunity to equate the struggle for the Union with what was
best in the nation. In *Specimen Days*, even a column of troops
would remind him of "the majesty and reality of the American people *en masse*." But for Melville the opposite impulse
was now at work. In "The House-top," the poem that Alfred
Kazin rightly describes as the most personal in *Battle-Pieces*,
Melville took as his subject the antidraft riots that in June,

48. McWilliams, *The Idea of Fraternity in America*, 328–71.
49. *Moby Dick*, 160. On the violence and expansionist nature of Jacksonianism, see Michael Paul Rogin, *Fathers and Children: Andrew Jackson
and the Subjugation of the American Indian* (New York, 1975), 296–313.

1863, raged in New York City for four days and required five regiments from the Army of the Potomac to put down. The picture Melville offers of wartime America is one in which the crowd represents the nation at its worst. In "The House-top" we see New York dominated by a population of "ship-rats" who spread "the Atheist roar of riot." The democracy they stand for is in direct contradiction to that of the "Re-public's faith," and in the end, all that saves the city from worse destruction is "black artillery." There is no chance that this crowd will ever discipline itself or spark the admiration Whitman expressed for New York in his "Mannahatta" of 1860, where he celebrated the "crowded streets" filled with "a million people—manners free and superb."[50]

With "The House-top," however, Melville was still not through writing about the crowd. In his posthumously pub-lished *Billy Budd*, he turned again to the crowd, this time creating a story that might easily have ended in a repeat of the *Town-Ho's* mutiny. Set in 1797, when the British navy was plagued by rebellions at Spithead and Nore, *Billy Budd* is the tale of a sailor who is forced to join a British warship, falsely accused of disloyalty, and hanged after he accidentally kills his accuser. Billy is a true innocent, and after his death the crew of the warship onto which he has been impressed makes a move toward rebellion. But in *Billy Budd*, no insurrection takes place, no Steelkit steps forward to assert leadership. The crew remains a vague "multitude," and Melville keeps his tale centered on the political conscience of Captain Vere, for whom the crowd and the egalitarian impulses it represents are anath-ema. The result is a historical perspective that suggests, as Alan Trachtenberg argues in *The Incorporation of America*, that in *Billy Budd*, Melville may well have been responding to the mass unrest that affected industrial America in both 1877 and 1886.[51] But what is clear beyond speculation is that more than thirty years after *Moby Dick*, Melville has taken the

50. Mark Van Doren (ed.), *The Portable Walt Whitman* (New York, 1976), 442; Alfred A. Kazin, *An American Procession* (New York, 1984), 121. On the political implications of the 1863 draft riots in New York, see David Montgom-ery, *Beyond Equality: Labor and the Radical Republicans, 1862–1872* (Ur-bana, 1981), 101–108.

51. Herman Melville, *Billy Budd, Sailor (An Inside Narrative)*, ed. Har-rison Hayford and Merton M. Sealts, Jr. (Chicago, 1962), 127–28. See Alan

dangers he previously attributed to the majority crowd and applied them to the kind of crowd once exempt from his criticism.

Mark Twain would certainly have appreciated such political pessimism. For Twain, crowd rule—above all, that of the lynch mob—was inseparable from slavery. He knew, as his *Autobiography* makes clear, that the newspapers and the churches could make slavery seem respectable ("the local newspapers said nothing against it; the local pulpit taught us that God approved it"), but in his eyes it was the crowd in the form of a lynch mob that provided the ultimate guarantee that slavery would be maintained in the antebellum South. In *Huckleberry Finn* the crowd that pursues Jim and wants to hang him as an example to other runaway slaves is in its "lawless lawfulness" an extension of the southern justice system and southern mores.[52]

Twain did not have to exaggerate facts to create this picture of an antebellum mob. In a society in which all white men were legally authorized to seize runaway slaves, nothing could unite plantation owners and small farmers more quickly than the kind of rumor Tom Sawyer starts in *Huckleberry Finn*, when he sends the Phelpses a note saying there is a conspiracy afoot to set Jim free. The ultimate southern fear, as David Potter has argued in *The South and Sectional Conflict*, was of a slave uprising brought about by antislavery men, and anything hinting at such a possibility was enough to cause panic. In portraying the South this way, Twain was, however, doing much more than exposing the recent past. He was also addressing volatile racial issues in the America in which he was living. The Compromise of 1877, which had given the presidency to Rutherford B. Hayes in exchange for the end of Reconstruction, was just eight years old when *Huckleberry Finn* was published. The postwar South was being "redeemed" by men who believed the best way to unite whites was through

Trachtenberg, *The Incorporation of America: Culture and Society in the Gilded Age* (New York, 1982), 202–207.

52. Mark Twain, *Autobiography* (2 vols.; New York, 1929), I, 101. On the conservative mob and "lawless lawfulness," see Richard Maxwell Brown, *Strain of Violence* (New York, 1975), 91–179.

the systematic repression of blacks. In the year *Huckleberry Finn* appeared, one could already see the kinds of Jim Crow laws and a rise in lynching that by the turn of the century would lead to segregation throughout the slave states and over one hundred black deaths per year at the hands of mobs.[53]

In *The Silent South*, George Washington Cable, with whom Mark Twain would travel the lecture circuit in 1885, would write of this new racism and violence, "America has no room for a state of society which makes its lower classes harmless by abridging their liberties, or, as one of the favored class lately said to me, has 'got 'em so they don't give no trouble.'" In Cable's view, such a "humiliating and tyrannous" system menaced recovery from the war.[54] Twain agreed with this judgment, and when we turn to *Huckleberry Finn*, we see a social vision as contemporary as Cable's. All that is missing from *Huckleberry Finn* are the explicit analogies between past and present Twain made in *Life on the Mississippi* when he compared the South of the 1880s to the South he had known before the Civil War.

Twain was not, however, above making such analogies in his fiction, and one of the best ways of putting the crowd in *Huckleberry Finn* in perspective is to begin with a look at *A Connecticut Yankee in King Arthur's Court*. In *Connecticut Yankee*, the crowd always acts in a bullying, brutal fashion. It attacks the king and the Yankee when they are disguised as "petty" freemen with the same alacrity that it stones a defenseless woman until she "hardly looked human." For Twain, these assaults are only a starting point. When we turn to his chapter "The Tragedy of the Manor House," we see that he reserves his most serious attention for what he regards as a political contradiction: the crowd's loyalty to a system that offers it little. This chapter begins at night with the king and the Yankee taking shelter in the home of a farmer. The next

53. Kenneth Stampp, *The Peculiar Institution* (New York, 1956), 140, 153; David Potter, *The South and the Sectional Conflict* (Baton Rouge, 1968), 78–80; C. Vann Woodward, *Origins of the New South, 1877–1913* (Baton Rouge, 1951), 51–74, 212–34; C. Vann Woodward, *The Strange Career of Jim Crow* (New York, 1974), 67–109. For lynching figures, see Brown, *Strain of Violence*, 214–16.

54. George Washington Cable, *The Silent South* (Montclair, N.J., 1969), 16, 23.

afternoon, the farmer's wife tells them that on the night of their arrival the lord of the manor was found murdered and that her husband was "active with the mob" that avenged his death. As she continues her story, we realize that not only have the actual murderers escaped, but, on the basis of a rumor started by the murdered lord's servants, eighteen persons have been hanged or butchered. A mob composed of "the community in general" has not even waited to sort out the truth. It has joined in an instant crusade against a humble family assumed to be guilty because they were "lately treated with peculiar harshness" by the lord. How could the farmer's wife tell such a horrible story so calmly? How could a crowd so rapidly bring itself to murder? These are the questions that fascinate Twain, and soon after the farmer's wife completes her story, he breaks the flow of his narrative to have the Yankee comment, "The painful thing about all this business was, the alacrity with which this oppressed community had turned their cruel hands against their own class in the interest of the common oppressor. This man and woman seemed to feel that in a quarrel between a person of their own class and his lord, it was the natural and proper and rightful thing for that poor devil's whole caste to side with the master and fight his battle for him, without ever stopping to inquire into the rights or wrongs of the matter."[55]

The crowd's political reaction is depressing to the Yankee, who describes himself as "a man with the dream of a republic in his head," but he will not soften his observations by suggesting that such thinking is limited to the past. "It reminded me of a time, thirteen centuries away," he comments, "when the 'poor whites' of our South who were always despised, and frequently insulted, by the slave lords around them, and who owed their base condition simply to the presence of slavery in their midst, were yet pusillanimously ready to side with the slave lords in all political moves for the upholding and perpetuating of slavery, and did also finally shoulder their muskets and pour out their lives in an effort to prevent the destruction of that very institution which degraded them."[56]

55. Mark Twain, *A Connecticut Yankee in King Arthur's Court,* ed. Bernard L. Stein (Berkeley, 1984), 252, 353, 295–96, 297.
56. *Ibid.,* 297.

The Yankee's comments reflect the paradox Kenneth Stampp describes in *The Peculiar Institution* when he observes that, although the South's independent yeomanry were hurt by slavery, they persisted in defending it and could always be counted on to join "the mobs which sporadically dealt summary justice to lawless slaves." The Yankee's comments are also an introduction to *Huckleberry Finn*, in which the southern lynch mobs draw from all quarters, save the most aristocratic, of white society. The first crowd we encounter, the Bricksville mob that wants to hang Colonel Sherburn for shooting Boggs, contains "a mighty onery lot," the town loafers. But in addition to the loafers, the crowd is composed of respectable people, families who have come from the country to spend the day in Bricksville. When Boggs is dying, the whole town gathers around him for a morbid last look. Twain, like Hawthorne and Melville before him, will not write off his crowds by ascribing their behavior to a lower-class mentality.[57]

When we trace the development of the Bricksville mob, we see a close correspondence to Twain's later observation (made in the Vienna library of Krafft-Ebing) that "lynch law means mob-lawlessness . . . it argues that men in a crowd do not act as they would as individuals. In a crowd they don't think for themselves, but become impregnated by contagious sentiments uppermost in the minds of all who happen to be en masse."[58] At the start of the Bricksville section, the town is no more than a scattered group of people having a good time. They do not show signs of coming together as a mob, and when Colonel Sherburn says he will shoot Boggs if he is insulted again, the response from those who hear the threat is a compassionate one. They stop laughing and become very sober. Just before the shooting, a number of townspeople even do their best to keep things from getting out of hand. Some try to quiet Boggs down, and one person goes to fetch his daughter in the hope that she can keep him from cursing Sherburn.[59]

57. Stampp, *The Peculiar Institution,* 428; Twain, *Huckleberry Finn,* 181, 183, 187.

58. Twain's remarks, made in conversation, are reported in Henry W. Fisher, *Abroad with Mark Twain and Eugene Field* (New York, 1922), 59. See also Walter Blair, "The French Revolution and *Huckleberry Finn,*" *Modern Philology,* XXV (August, 1957), 21–35.

59. Twain, *Huckleberry Finn,* 185.

The shooting changes everything. Like a Pavlovian bell, it sets off a series of responses that seem to have a life of their own. The town turns into a crowd and the crowd into a southern version of the kind of raging mob that dominates Carlyle's *French Revolution*. Once Boggs is shot, bloodthirsty curiosity rather than compassion becomes the order of the day. Boggs and his daughter are practically smothered by onlookers as "the crowd closed up around them, and shouldered and jammed one another, with their necks, trying to see." When Boggs dies a moment later, all civility stops, as Huck's description makes clear. "Well pretty soon the whole town was there, squirming and scrouging and pushing and shoving to get at the window and have a look, but people that had places wouldn't give them up, and folks behind them was saying all the time, 'Say, now, you've looked enough . . . other folks has their rights as well as you.'" At the end, "Everybody that seen the shooting was telling how it happened, and there was a big crowd packed around each one of those fellows, stretching their necks and listening."[60]

It is in this atmosphere of morbid curiosity and self-righteousness (Boggs is laid to rest with "one large Bible under his head" and another "on his breast"), when "the streets was full, and everybody was excited," that someone in the crowd says, "Sherburn ought to be lynched," and the explosion Twain's scene has been moving toward takes place. Whatever personal decency or individuality the townspeople of Bricksville may have is lost in the rush to lynch Sherburn. As Huck observes, "In about a minute everybody was saying it; so away they went, mad and yelling, and snatching down every clothes line they come to to do the hanging with." The crowd now has a momentum and a personality of its own, and as it proceeds to Colonel Sherburn's house it sweeps everything and everyone before it. Blacks, of course, do not dare join in, and women and children are secondary figures, but the white, masculine composition of the crowd does not change the fact that it embodies the ruling values of Bricksville and encounters no opposition.

60. The link between Twain and Carlyle is developed in Walter Blair, *Mark Twain and Huck Finn* (Berkeley, 1960), 310–14; Twain, *Huckleberry Finn*, 187.

They swarmed up towards Sherburn's house, a-whooping and raging like Injuns, and everything had to clear the way or get run over and tromped to mush, and it was awful to see. Children was heeling it ahead of the mob, screaming and trying to get out of the way; and every window along the road was full of women's heads, and there was nigger boys in every tree, and bucks and wenches looking over every fence; and as soon as the mob would get nearly to them they would break and skaddle back out of reach. Lots of the women and girls was crying and taking on, scared most to death.[61]

All that remains after this scene is for Twain to show what crowd bravery amounts to, and this he does by having the mob's intended victim, Colonel Sherburn, defend himself. Never, interestingly, does Sherburn try to justify his shooting of Boggs. He simply faces down his accusers, making them see that their collectivity is born of individual weakness and momentary hysteria. Sherburn begins by staring down anyone in the crowd who dares look at him, and then he points out the crowd's need for a weak victim. "The idea of *you* lynching anybody! It's amusing," he sarcastically observes. "Because you're brave enough to tar and feather poor friendless cast-out women that come along here, did you think you had grit enough to lay your hands on a *man?*" Sherburn does not stop here. Once he has exposed the crowd's cowardice, he goes on to point out to them that it is anonymity they depend on. "Your mistake is, that you didn't bring a man with you; that's one mistake, and the other is that you didn't come in the dark and fetch your masks." Any real lynching, Sherburn concludes, "will be done in the dark, southern fashion; and when they come they'll bring their masks."[62]

By the end of his confrontation with the Bricksville mob, Sherburn is treating them as if they were an 1830s version of the Ku Klux Klan, telling them that they don't like what they are doing but don't know how to retreat when "half a man" like Buck Harkness works them up. "You're afraid to back down—afraid you'll be found out to be what you are—*cowards*—and so you raise a yell . . . and come raging up here, swearing what big things you're going to do," Sherburn says. He concludes, "The pitifulest thing out is a mob; that's what

61. Twain, *Huckleberry Finn*, 187, 188, 189.
62. *Ibid.*, 190, 191.

an army is—a mob; they don't fight with courage that's born
in them but with courage that's borrowed from their mass,
and from their officers. But a mob without any *man* at the
head of it is *beneath* pitifulness. Now the thing for *you* to do
is to droop your tails and go home and crawl in a hole." A band
of men once likened to Indians have now been reduced to bur-
rowing animals who live underground, and they accept this
final characterization. They leave when Sherburn, whom they
have wanted to kill, tells them to go, and their departure re-
verses the traditional sea imagery of a mob as a rising tide.
"The crowd washed back sudden, and then broke all apart,
and went tearing off every which way, and Buck Harkness he
heeled it after them, looking tolerable cheap."[63]

For Twain, the one problem with the Bricksville section of
Huckleberry Finn is Sherburn himself. The qualities that
make Sherburn so articulate and contemptuous of the crowd
that wants to hang him also make him an unfeeling, unsympathetic figure. It is not until Huck arrives at the Phelpses'
farm that the grim consequences of a crowd getting its way
are shown, and Twain makes us see that even such frauds as
the duke and the dauphin are worthy of sympathy when they
become the victims of a mob. This time there is no analysis of
the mob, only Huck's description, followed by his response to
the humiliation of the duke and the dauphin:

> As we struck into the town . . . here comes a raging rush of people
> with torches, and an awful whooping and yelling, and yelling, and
> banging tin pans and blowing horns; and we jumped to one side to
> let them go by; and as they went by I see they had the king and the
> duke astraddle of a rail—that is, I know it *was* the king and duke,
> though they was all over tar and feathers, and didn't look like
> nothing in the world that was human—just looked like a couple of
> monstrous big soldier-plumes. Well, it made me sick to see it; and I
> was sorry for them poor pitiful rascals, it seemed like I couldn't
> ever feel any hardness against them any more in the world. It was a
> dreadful thing to see. Human beings *can* be awful to one another.

This scene provides a crucial link to the final chapters of
Huckleberry Finn, where Jim is the victim of a crowd of farmers. For if men as unworthy as the duke and the dauphin are

63. *Ibid.*, 190–91.

pathetic as the victims of a mob, what remains to be said when Jim is put in such a position?[64]

Kenneth Stampp has written, "The angry mobs who dealt extra-legal justice to slaves accused of serious crimes committed barbarities seldom matched by the most brutal masters."[65] Certainly Twain had as much in mind when in the final chapters of *Huckleberry Finn* he allowed Tom Sawyer to frighten the Phelpses and their neighbors into thinking Jim was going to get free with outside help. Like the mobs we have already seen, the farmers who gather at the Phelpses' home are an angry bunch of men. But in their case their anger is formidable. What distinguishes them from the townspeople who wanted to lynch Colonel Sherburn and who succeeded in tarring and feathering the duke and the dauphin is their uniform respectability and seriousness. This is not a spontaneous crowd that has come into existence to have a good time. It is an organized crowd prepared to act.

Huck takes one look at the farmers who have come to prevent Jim from escaping and realizes Tom's game has gotten out of hand. "I opened the door and walked into the setting room. My, but there was a crowd there! Fifteen farmers and everyone of them had a gun. I was most powerful sick, and slunk to a chair and set down." For Huck, however, who has already seen two mobs in action, there is little he can do. What these farmers imagine they are avenging is not a minor wrong or the murder of the town drunkard but an attack on the slave system. In their minds they are a vigilance committee.[66]

As it turns out, the pursuit of Jim ends on a happy note. Jim is recaptured after he passes up his chance to escape by stopping to help Tom Sawyer, who has been wounded by a stray bullet. Then he is set free by the terms of Miss Watson's will. (She has, we learn from Tom, died while Jim and Huck were going down the Mississippi.) But this happy ending is pure literary contrivance. It does not seem convincing, nor does it erase the grim implications that arise when Jim tries to escape and the farmers go after him. As soon as Jim is brought back to the Phelpses' farm, a number of the men want to make

64. *Ibid.*, 290.
65. Stampp, *The Peculiar Institution*, 190.
66. Twain, *Huckleberry Finn*, 336.

him a scapegoat and lynch him on the spot. "The men was very huffy," Huck notes, "and some of them wanted to hang Jim for an example to all the other niggers around there, so they wouldn't be trying to run away like Jim done, and making such a raft of trouble, and keeping a whole family scared most to death for days and nights." What saves Jim is not compassion on the part of the crowd but their awareness of his market value and the fear, as several farmers put it, that "his owner would turn up and make us pay for him."[67]

Jim is still beaten and cursed, and when the doctor who has removed the bullet from Tom Sawyer's leg reports that Jim gave up his freedom to help Tom, he merely advises the crowd, "Don't be no rougher on him than you're obliged to, because he ain't a bad nigger." The doctor knows that Jim can never be forgiven for trying to escape, and so do the men who have him in tow. Their response to the doctor's story about him is to promise "they wouldn't cuss him no more." Huck hopes they will also make Jim's confinement easier, but he quickly realizes that given the crowd's mood, such an idea is wishful thinking. "I hoped they was going to say he could have one or two of the chains took off, because they was rotten heavy, or could have meat and greens with his bread and water; but they didn't think of it, and I reckoned it warn't best for me to mix in." As Twain knew, a respectable southern crowd would balk at killing an escaped slave, but it could never put aside the fear and resentment such bids for freedom aroused.[68]

Huck's only alternative is to head for the territory "ahead of the rest." The fraternal community he and Jim achieved on their raft has no future within the political confines of American society, and when we look at Twain's portrait of postbellum society, Huck's decision seems prophetic. The America of Twain's *The Gilded Age* is totally corrupt, and the America that he depicts in his 1901 essay "The United States of Lyncherdom" is worse. It is a country in which, as John Hope Franklin observed in *From Slavery to Freedom*, "rioting in

67. *Ibid.*, 352.
68. *Ibid.*, 352, 353, 354. For a discussion of how the value of a slave prevented lynchings during a period when there was tremendous fear and anger over runaways, see Eugene Genovese, *Roll, Jordan, Roll: The World the Slaves Made* (New York, 1974), 32, 48, 613–19.

the North was as vicious and almost as prevalent as in the South." In "The United States of Lyncherdom," Twain sounds like his own Colonel Sherburn when he asks, "Why does a crowd . . . pretend to enjoy a lynching? Why does it lift no hand or voice in protest?" At this point, Twain has no answer except that men are cowards and crowds bring out their most cowardly instincts. "Each man is afraid of his neighbor's disapproval—a thing which, to the general run of the race, is more dreaded than wounds or death," he insists. If there is a difference between Twain and Colonel Sherburn, it is that by the turn of the century Twain was more pessimistic about where the "mania" of lynching and mob rule would lead. "I may live," he concluded, "to see a negro burned in Union Square, New York, with fifty thousand people present, and not a sheriff visible, not a governor, not a constable, not a clergyman, not a law-and-order representative of any sort."[69]

This view of the crowd is consistent with the picture of the avenging mob that rules such twentieth-century fiction as Walter Van Tilburg Clark's *The Ox-Bow Incident*, William Faulkner's *Intruder in the Dust*, and Richard Wright's "Big Boy Leaves Home." Twain's final portrait of the crowd remains, nonetheless, a direct extension of the vision of the preindustrial crowd that dominates the classic American novel. It is no accident that his heroes, like those of Hawthorne and Melville, consistently find themselves the victims of crowds, even the crowds they briefly join. The America all three authors were born into was an America whose collective energies had been set free by the Revolution. For them, however, there was no nineteenth-century equivalent of the Revolution and the crowds it spawned. The Jacksonian labor movement and the struggle for the ten-hour workday never captured their imagination, and the Civil War seemed to them anything but a glorious collective hour.[70]

As a result, Hawthorne, Melville, and Twain could not put

69. Twain, *Huckleberry Finn*, 362; John Hope Franklin, *From Slavery to Freedom* (New York, 1965), 435; Mark Twain, "The United States of Lyncherdom," in Maxwell Geismar (ed.), *Mark Twain and the Three R's* (Indianapolis, 1973), 37, 35.

70. See Edward Pessen, *Most Uncommon Jacksonians: The Radical Leaders of the Early Labor Movement* (Albany, 1967), 3–51, 197–203.

aside their belief that in the America they knew, democratic men acting as a crowd were time and again a danger to the freedom and independence of democratic man. This did not mean, as has so often been argued, that Hawthorne, Melville, and Twain stopped looking closely at society. Given their democratic instincts, however, it did mean that writing about American political life was always painful for them. Whitman's mystical approach to the crowd—in which the many prove the salvation of the one, and the aggregate and the individual are reconciled—did not reflect reality as Hawthorne, Melville, and Twain saw it, nor did it offer a solution they were willing to incorporate into their fiction.[71] There was, so far as they were concerned, no getting around the fact that, in a nation committed to majority rule, the majority crowd constituted a unique, potentially cannibalistic menace, and from this paradox a final troubling conclusion followed: in America the individualism and egalitarianism they most admired were safest when political action stayed at a minimum, when democratic men kept their distance from democratic man.

71. See Larzer Ziff, "Whitman and the Crowd," *Critical Inquiry*, X (June, 1984), 589–90.

III

Class and Crowd in American Fiction

For the social realists, whose fiction so brilliantly captured the turmoil of American life from the late nineteenth century through the Great Depression, the crowd was no less central an issue than it was for the classic American novelist. For the social realists, however, the crowd in question was working class in origin. What this crowd put to the test was whether these writers' concern for the poor could be made compatible with their worries over what class warfare could do to the country. Never far from their minds were the kinds of fears Jack London—his socialism notwithstanding—raised in *The Iron Heel,* in which he imagined the poor rising up as "a mob, an awful river" of "great hairy beasts," all "roaring for the blood of their masters."[1]

The dilemma posed by such fears was one Abraham Lincoln was forced to confront during the final years of his presidency. When we take as a point of reference his 1864 "Reply to a Committee from the Workingmen's Association of New York," we see how difficult it was from the Civil War on for anyone in the public eye to reach a "balanced" perspective on the working-class crowd. Lincoln's answer to the workingmen reflects nothing so much as his uneasiness at having to address them at all. At the start he is quick to point out that the continuation of slavery amounts to "a war upon the rights of all working people," and then, quoting from an earlier speech, he moves on to a timeless defense of labor. "Labor is," he declares, "the superior of capital, and deserves much the higher consideration." We live in a world where "the strongest bond of human sympathy, outside of the family relation, should be

1. Jack London, *The Iron Heel* (New York, 1924), 326–27. London borrowed imagery from the San Francisco fire and earthquake to describe the crowd. See Andrew Sinclair, *Jack: A Biography of Jack London* (New York, 1977), 137–40.

one uniting all working people," he insists. But after showering this praise on labor, Lincoln changes his tone dramatically. Memory of the role working-class crowds took in the New York antidraft riots of 1863 is still fresh in his mind, and he concludes his address with a stern admonition. "Let not him who is houseless pull down the house of another," Lincoln warns, "but let him work diligently and build one for himself, thus by example assuring that his own shall be safe from violence when built."[2]

When we turn to the fiction of America's social realists, we find this same cautionary note sounded by such middle-class observers as William Dean Howells' Basil March and John Steinbeck's Doc Burton. Even in Theodore Dreiser's *Sister Carrie,* where crowd violence proves effective, those who are responsible for it observe implicit restraints. But what is most revealing about the portrait of the working-class crowd that Howells, Dreiser, and Steinbeck offer is that the questions their portrayals raise about the relationship between violence and social change are not limited to the violence the crowd initiates. In their novels, the perspective of those at the bottom of society is never forgotten, and over and over we are made to see what the working-class crowd is up against.[3] The brutalizing industrialism that has made the crowd necessary is its justification. But this same industrialism is also the crowd's worst enemy, for it has brought about a society whose most powerful men, those who control productivity, are opposed to all but the most feeble working-class protest.

If we are to come to terms with the tradition of social realism represented in America by such politically self-conscious fiction as Howells' *A Hazard of New Fortunes,* Dreiser's *Sister Carrie,* and Steinbeck's *In Dubious Battle* and *The Grapes of Wrath,* we must weigh the sympathy these books show for the working poor along with the changing picture they offer of the working-class crowd in action. Nothing less will do. In

2. Abraham Lincoln, "Reply to a Committee from the Workingmen's Association of New York," in John G. Nicolay and John Hay (eds.), *Complete Works of Abraham Lincoln* (12 vols.; New York, 1905), X, 50–54.
3. On writing history from this perspective, see Jesse Lemisch, "The American Revolution from the Bottom Up," in Barton J. Bernstein (ed.), *Towards a New Past: Dissenting Essays in American History* (New York, 1968), 3–6.

these novels, the crowd is the most powerful political vehicle that workers have. In turn, how they behave as a crowd—whether they move from spontaneous to disciplined protest, whether in the course of striking they develop leaders of their own, whether they achieve a sense of unity—determines how they are to be judged: if they are to be pitied and sentimentalized or seen as capable of changing their lives collectively.[4]

We find the first in-depth picture in American literature of a working-class crowd in *A Hazard of New Fortunes*. Published in 1890, Howells' novel reflects the labor turmoil of the 1880s, which saw 700,000 men go out in just one year and 10,000 strikes and lockouts over the course of the decade. For the rich in *A Hazard of New Fortunes*, memory of the nationwide railway strikes of 1877—and the fear John Hay expressed at the time, that "any hour the mob chooses it can destroy any city in the country"—is still fresh. But, for the working class of *A Hazard of New Fortunes*, reality is altogether different. The workers have neither the power nor the inclination to challenge the legitimacy of the state. Just striking is a desperate last resort for them. In a decade in which 40 percent of the American labor force made less than the five hundred dollars per year needed to support a family in minimal comfort, these workers are struggling to survive on wages that barely amount to a dollar a day.[5]

That by 1890 the genteel William Dean Howells would come to side with the working poor is not clear in his writings as late as 1885 or in his most successful novel, *The Rise of Silas Lapham*. From the second half of the decade on, however, Howells was a different writer. His reading of Tolstoy and acceptance of the latter's Christian socialism changed his sense of the novelist's role, and soon his fiction began to mirror the social concerns that had already altered his thinking.

4. On the varieties of crowd response, see George Rudé, *Paris and London in the Eighteenth Century* (New York, 1975), 18–22.

5. Alan Trachtenberg, *The Incorporation of America: Culture and Society in the Gilded Age* (New York, 1982), 89; John Hay quoted in Kenneth S. Lynn, *William Dean Howells: An American Life* (New York, 1971), 273; William Dean Howells, *A Hazard of New Fortunes* (New York, 1911), 486. On family income in the 1880s, see David Montgomery, "Labor in the Industrial Era," in Richard B. Morris (ed.), *The American Worker* (Washington, D.C., 1976), 117–18.

In *The Minister's Charge* (1886) and in *Annie Kilburn* (1888), he presented a picture of the poor that was far more graphic than anything he had done before. The turning point for Howells came with a very public event, the 1886 strike at the McCormick Reaper Works in Chicago. At a May 4 rally in Haymarket Square, a bomb was thrown at police dispersing a prostrike crowd, and in short order eight anarchists were arrested, tried, and, on the flimsiest of evidence, convicted of the crime. In Howells' judgment, it was a clear miscarriage of justice, and within a year he became involved in the controversy as did no other man in American letters.[6]

For Howells the public figure, the result of his activism was a series of stinging attacks from the press. But for Howells the author of *A Hazard of New Fortunes*, Haymarket Square was an invaluable lesson in the risks anyone took when he defended, let alone joined, a crowd seeking social justice. It now became more important than ever for him to link the world around him to the world of his fiction. In his preface to a later edition of *A Hazard of New Fortunes*, Howells observed that the novel "became, to my thinking, the most vital of my fictions, through my quickened interest in the life about me," and nothing bears out this assertion so well as the letters he wrote at the time. They are filled with references to the "civic murder" in Chicago and to the newspapers' biased treatment of strikes in general.[7]

The event that Howells used to express his feelings about Haymarket Square was, however, much closer to home. It was a New York streetcar strike that occurred shortly after he and his wife moved to the city from Boston. Again, Howells' retrospective preface provides the key to his thinking.

> The shedding of blood which is for the remission of sins had been symbolized by the bombs and scaffolds of Chicago, and the hearts

6. Larzer Ziff, *The American 1890s* (Lincoln, Neb., 1979), 32–40; Lynn, *William Dean Howells*, 288–91. Howells corresponded with Roger A. Pryor, attorney for the Chicago anarchists, and he also made a public appeal for clemency on their behalf in the New York *Tribune* (November 4, 1887). See Mildred Howells (ed.), *Life in Letters of William Dean Howells* (2 vols.; Garden City, 1928), I, 393–401.

7. Howells, *A Hazard of New Fortunes*, vi; Mildred Howells (ed.), *Life in Letters*, I, 401–403, 413; Henry Nash Smith and William M. Gibson (eds.), *Mark Twain–Howells Letters* (2 vols.; Cambridge, Mass., 1960), II, 597–99.

of those who felt the wrongs bound up with our rights . . . were thrilling with griefs and hopes hitherto strange to the average American breast. Opportunely for me there was a great street-car strike in New York, and the story began to find its way to issues nobler and larger than those of the love-affairs common to fiction.[8]

When we turn to the novel, it is apparent how deeply politics have told. The big crowd-strike scene provides the climax of the book and forever changes the personal and political lives of all the main characters in it. For Berthold Lindau, the European-born radical of *A Hazard of New Fortunes*, the strike is fatal. Lindau, who as a young man fought in the German Revolution of 1848 and lost an arm in the American Civil War, is clubbed to death by a policeman as he encourages the strikers on. But the strike is equally tragic for the man who most hates Lindau, Jacob Dryfoos, the conservative owner of the magazine Lindau and Basil March, the central figure in *A Hazard of New Fortunes*, work for. Dryfoos, who believes the strikers are a "parcel of lazy hounds" for whom "clubbing is too good" loses his son Conrad when Conrad goes to the scene of the strike to see if he can prevent violence and is shot. Only Basil March, who at the time of the strike occupies political territory safely between that of Lindau and Dryfoos, survives the events unscathed. But he too is changed by the bloodshed of the strike. By the end of the novel, he is a far more sensitive man than the liberal magazine editor who once observed, "What amuses me is to find that in an affair of this kind the roads [trolley or railroad lines] have rights and the strikers have rights, but the public has no rights at all."[9]

This change in March, whose formal political judgments provide a framework for *A Hazard of New Fortunes*, reflects the pivotal role of the crowd in Howells' novel and the care he took to make sure his climactic crowd scene did not become a deus ex machina for drawing together an otherwise loose sketch of New York in the 1880s. The novel hinges on the development of March's social consciousness, and because of his involvement in the streetcar strike, we see him evolve from a distant observer of the poor to a writer who admits that he belongs to a profession that contributes to their exploitation.

8. Howells, *A Hazard of New Fortunes*, vi.
9. *Ibid.*, 485, 474–75.

The first stage in March's development comes when he arrives in New York and must find a place to live. March, whose editorial career and move from Boston to New York parallel that of Howells, is overwhelmed by what he faces, and his initial response to the city is a combination of squeamishness and superiority. At first he agrees with his wife that all the streets are "ill-paved, dirty, and repulsive." But as he tours the city looking for an apartment to rent, March slowly begins to change. When his wife complains that a neighborhood their hack driver has taken them through is ugly, March sarcastically replies, "This driver may be a philanthropist in disguise . . . may want us to think about the people who are not merely carried through this street in a coupe, but have to spend their whole lives in it, winter and summer, with no hopes of driving out of it, except in a hearse." At this point, March is too new to the city to give up his belief that the poor feel their suffering less than the rich "because they've been used to it all their lives." Nonetheless, by the time he finds an apartment, March has changed sufficiently to look with chagrin on the period in his life when he didn't notice the poor and to say to his wife, "If it's the unhappy who see unhappiness, think what misery must be revealed to people who pass their lives in the really squalid tenement-house streets."[10] March's comment is still that of a writer who prefers to think of himself as innocent rather than *engagé*, but it foreshadows the conclusion of *A Hazard of New Fortunes*, in which March's vision of New York will be remarkably close to that of his real-life contemporary, Jacob Riis, in *How the Other Half Lives*.

The next stage in March's development comes when he begins to see the economic connection between those who have money and those who do not. The change in March is once again gradual, and his instinct is to resist the full implications of this new awareness. When Lindau asks him, "How much money can a man honestly earn without wronging or oppressing some other men?" March evades his question, saying, "I should say about five thousand dollars a year . . . because it's my experience that I could never earn more." March cannot, however, avoid learning how the rich profit at the expense of

10. *Ibid.*, 64, 70–71, 78.

the poor when he goes to a party at the home of Jacob Dryfoos. There he hears Dryfoos tell with pride how he, with the aid of a dozen Pinkertons, broke up the union his workers started and then made an agreement with other businessmen "not to employ any man who would not swear that he was non-union." The story is not enough to make March drop his association with Dryfoos' *Every Other Week*, as Lindau does. But the story does put him in an adversarial relationship with Dryfoos, and as in his earlier tenement experience, March emerges from this encounter with a more complex sense of the way society works. "Merely business standards" are, he tells his wife, so low that they cannot be of use when it comes to questions of principle.[11]

With this heightened awareness of the poor and of business ethics, March investigates the streetcar strike that will alter his and everyone else's life in *A Hazard of New Fortunes*. He is at first reluctant to get near the violence. When the manager of *Every Other Week* suggests that March cover the strike in the historical spirit of Defoe writing about the plague, he asks, "Will you undertake to make it right with Mrs. March if I'm killed, and she and the children are not killed with me?" March nonetheless finds himself drawn to the strike, and as this happens the liberal perspective he has tried to maintain becomes harder and harder to keep. No sooner does the strike begin than the one neutral force, the State Board of Arbitration, is rendered useless by the streetcar companies. While the workers are quick to submit their grievances to the board, "the roads were as one road in declaring that there was nothing to arbitrate and that they were merely asserting their right to manage their own affairs in their own way."[12]

This turn of events prompts March to comment, "The roads and strikers are allowed to fight out a private war in our midst—as thoroughly and precisely a private war as any we despise the Middle Ages for having tolerated . . . and we stand by like sheep and wait till they get tired." But the minute March experiences the strike directly, his tone changes. The workers he observes are "quiet, decent-looking people"—

11. *Ibid.*, 219, 395, 413.
12. *Ibid.*, 477, 474.

the type of sober union men Robert Koehler depicts so sympathetically in his 1886 painting *The Strike*. As he watches them standing on a streetcorner in their "simple Sunday best," March "could well believe that they had nothing to do with the riotous outbreaks in other parts of the city." By contrast, the police who ride alongside the strikebreakers make a wholly different impression on March. When March tries to engage one of them in conversation, he is met with silent hostility, and only by great effort on his part does he remain the neutral journalist he wants to be. The policeman's attitude "gave him a fine sense of the ferocity which he had read of the French troops putting on towards the populace just before the coup d'état; he began to feel like the populace, but he struggled with himself and regained his character of philosophical observer."[13]

In this ambivalent mood, March stays on the streetcar he is riding and goes past his stop to the place where the strikers and the police have been clashing. March is not the only one drawn to this spot. Conrad Dryfoos is also headed here. Like March, he does not want to take sides, and he also has misgivings about the workers' strategy. "I think they were very foolish to strike—at this time, when the Elevated roads can do the work," he tells his father. Conrad is, however, unwilling to remain above the battle. He is convinced that the workers "have a righteous cause." He declares, "I pity them. My whole heart is with those poor men," and goes to the scene of the strike to do whatever he can to stop the fighting.[14]

At this point, the climactic crowd scene of *A Hazard of New Fortunes* takes place. The passage describing the violence, like the violence itself, is brief. One moment the street is quiet, the next moment "a tumult of shouting, cursing, struggling men" attack a streetcar.

> The driver was lashing his horses forward, and a policeman was at their heads, with the conductor pulling them; stones, clubs, brickbats hailed upon the car, the horses, the men trying to move them. The mob closed upon them in a body, and then a patrol wagon whirled up from the other side, and a squad of policemen leaped

13. *Ibid.*, 475, 479, 480.
14. *Ibid.*, 486, 487.

out and began to club the rioters. . . . They struck them under the
rims of their hats; the blows on the skulls sounded as if they had
fallen on stone; the rioters ran in all directions.

The riot is over almost as soon as it begins. By comparison to
the police, the workers are badly organized and ill prepared to
deal with violence. They throw brickbats and stones, which
do little damage. The police, on the other hand, fight with calculation. It is a textbook case of a working-class crowd taking
on more than it bargained for and then being overwhelmed.
Were we to look at this scene without remembering all that
led up to it, we would have grounds for considering Howells
unsympathetic to the workers he describes.[15]

Such is not the case, however. The sympathy that Howells
has built up for the streetcar drivers through Basil March's and
Conrad Dryfoos' observations is continued rather than ended
with this scene. Howells' picture is quite different from the
leading New York newspapers' descriptions of strikers as the
"howling mob" and "ignorant rabble with hungry mouths."
Although Howells does nothing to conceal the strikers' violence, he does not dwell on it. We do not see the consequences
of their decision to fight back. The "stones, clubs, brickbats"
that they throw "hailed upon the car, the horses, the men trying to move them." But never does a horse or a man bleed or
show pain. It is the blows struck by the police that we hear,
and it is the disproportionate force of their counterattack (the
workers throw stones and are in turn beaten upon as if they
were stone) that we notice. When Lindau, one-armed and
aged, arrives on the corner and begins shouting at the police,
his being struck down by an officer comes as no surprise. The
attack on Lindau in fact sets up what happens next, the shooting of Conrad Dryfoos.

> The officer whirled his club, and the old man threw his left arm up
> to shield his head. Conrad recognized Lindau, and now he saw the
> empty sleeve dangle in the air, over the stump of his wrist. He
> heard a shot in that turmoil beside the car, and something seemed
> to strike him in the breast. He was going to say to the policeman,
> "Don't strike him! He's an old soldier. You see he has no hand!"
> but he could not speak, he could not move his tongue. The police-

15. *Ibid.*, 491.

man stood there; he saw his face; it was not bad, not cruel; it was like the face of a statue, fixed, perdurable, a mere image of irresponsible and involuntary authority. Then Conrad fell forward, pierced through the heart by that shot fired from the car.[16]

Who fired the shot? Striker or policeman? Howells does not say. As in the case of the Haymarket Square bomb, the question of responsibility is never answered. With the shooting we are, however, immediately thrust back into a strike era in which, as labor historian David Montgomery has observed, "the most common cause of bloodshed was soldiers' firing into a crowd." Everything in this climactic scene is weighted in favor of the crowd of strikers. Even the statuelike policeman who confronts Conrad is almost a carbon copy of the officer who on the first day of the strike coldly observed, "I guess we shan't have to shoot much . . . we can drive the whole six thousand of them into the East River without pullin' a trigger."[17]

The most crucial judgment of the crowd in *A Hazard of New Fortunes* remains, however, that of Basil March. From what he has seen, March is not convinced that "love of justice" can excuse "sympathy with violence," but his contact with the crowd does shock him into still greater self-awareness and political sensitivity. Of Lindau he comments, "I could almost say he had earned the right to be wrong. He's a man of the most generous instincts, and a high ideal of justice, of equity—too high to be considered by a policeman with a club in his hand." And of himself and Conrad Dryfoos, March observes, "I was there in the cause of literary curiosity. . . . But Conrad—yes, he had some business there: it was his business to suffer there for the sins of others." Most important of all, the violence of the crowd scene pushes March to the point that he is willing to drop his irony and talk in the most passionate terms about social justice. "What I object to is this economic chance world in which we live," he tells his wife.

16. For comments from these and other newspapers, see Philip S. Foner, *History of the Labor Movement in the United States* (4 vols.; New York, 1972), I, 468–69; Howells, *A Hazard of New Fortunes*, 491–92.

17. David Montgomery, "Strikes in Nineteenth-Century America," *Social Science History*, IV (February, 1980), 89; Howells, *A Hazard of New Fortunes*, 471.

It ought to be law as inflexible in human affairs as the order of day
and night in the physical world, that if a man will work he shall
both rest and eat, and shall not be harassed with any question as to
how his repose and provision shall come. Nothing less ideal than
this satisfies the reason. But in our state of things no one is secure
of this. No one is sure of finding work; no one is sure of not losing
it. . . . And so we go on, pushing and pulling, climbing and crawl-
ing, thrusting aside and trampling underfoot.

March also admits that he has not yet reached the point of
living by this vision, but what is crucial is the change March
has undergone. March would never have thought to speak this
way earlier in *A Hazard of New Fortunes,* and his outburst reminds us once again of Howells' reaction to the Haymarket
Square controversy. The parallel between the two men is striking, as a letter from Howells to Hamlin Garland shows.

You'll easily believe that I did not bring myself to the point of
openly befriending those men who were civically murdered in
Chicago for their opinions without thinking and feeling much,
and my horizons have been indefinitely widened by the process. . . .
The new commonwealth must be founded in justice even to the
unjust, in generosity . . . and insure to every man the food and
shelter which the gift of life implies the right to. . . . I am reading
and thinking about questions that carry me beyond myself and my
miserable literary idolatries of the past; perhaps you'll find that
I've been writing about them. I am still the slave of selfishness,
but I no longer am content to be so. That's as far as I can honestly
say I've got.[18]

In the end, neither Howells nor March can do away with all
his fears, but then neither of these passages is written to suggest we must break completely with the past or not at all.
These passages address the feelings of writers who have come
to understand the desperation of the working poor and to
question their own position in a world where a Jacob Dryfoos
"could watch his money breed more money and bring greater
increase of its kind in an hour of luck than the toil of a thousand men could earn in a year."[19]

18. Howells, *A Hazard of New Fortunes,* 525, 500, 525, 507; Howells to
Hamlin Garland, January 15, 1888, in Mildred Howells (ed.), *Life in Letters,* I,
407–408.
19. Howells, *A Hazard of New Fortunes,* 303.

Howells would never again be the pious editor who once praised a favorite *Atlantic* contributor for teaching "the poor how a capitalist may be necessarily their friend," and in subsequent fiction he would remain loyal to the lessons of *A Hazard of New Fortunes.* This did not mean that Howells imagined prolonged class warfare ushering in the America his striking streetcar drivers need or that, in the fashion of Ignatius Donnelly in *Caesar's Column* and Jack London in *The Iron Heel,* he saw a value in apocalyptic scare novels in which the reader was made to see what a crowd of the poor might do if driven to the point of desperation. The just society Basil March envisions in the wake of Conrad Dryfoos' death seemed worthy of calmer treatment than that to Howells, and in the manner of Edward Bellamy in *Looking Backward,* Howells turned instead to utopian solutions, offering in *A Traveler from Altruria* and *Through the Eye of the Needle* the example of a country that replaced the "old competitive and monopolistic forms" with "the dream of brotherly equality."[20]

The social vision of Altruria was, as Ellen Moers has noted, one that Theodore Dreiser found especially appealing, and in the years before and after he wrote *Sister Carrie,* he turned to Howells for approval. Dreiser was not at all hesitant about courting Howells. In two articles, "How William Dean Howells Climbed Fame's Ladder" and "The Real Howells," Dreiser offered flattering public tribute to the man who had become the Dean of American Letters. In their private correspondence, Dreiser was even more laudatory, comparing Howells to Tolstoy and Thomas Hardy and concluding, "Of you three however I should not be able to choose, the spirit in each seeming to be the same."[21]

20. Howells quoted in Lynn, *William Dean Howells,* 277. It is significant that in *Caesar's Column* and *The Iron Heel,* the poor, whether led by "The Brotherhood of Destruction" or "The People of the Abyss," are unable to control their rage and in turn create a situation in which authoritarian governments are temporarily able to take advantage of the chaos they create. Ignatius Donnelly, *Caesar's Column* (Cambridge, Mass., 1960), 256–58, 280–84, 294–98; London, *The Iron Heel,* 324–28; William Dean Howells, *A Traveler from Altruria* (New York, 1978), 182, 194. See also John Thomas, *Alternative America* (Cambridge, Mass., 1983), 237–61.

21. Dreiser to William Dean Howells, May 14, 1902, in Ellen Moers, *Two Dreisers* (New York, 1969), 174–75.

Howells, however, could not bring himself to sponsor Dreiser's view of the working-class crowd. The political differences between the two writers are in part a reflection of the changes that occurred in America between the 1880s and the turn of the century. Howells' shock at the Haymarket Square controversy is understandable as is his belief that the working-class crowd should never resort to violence. For Dreiser in 1900, however, such innocence is out of the question. *Sister Carrie* is the product of a Dreiser who would not be shocked by the Homestead Lockout and reflects the fact that in the 1890s an experienced American labor movement faced not only a frontal assault by employers but also, as David Montgomery has pointed out, the systematic use of armed might by the government.[22]

It is Dreiser's experience as a journalist that most accounts for the differences between *Sister Carrie* and *A Hazard of New Fortunes*. Unlike Howells, who in the late 1880s was just becoming sensitized to the labor wars going on around him, Dreiser had no such initiation to go through when he went to write *Sister Carrie*. He had been in Pittsburgh a year after the Homestead Lockout and observed the "depressing" effect the Carnegie Steel Company's victory had on the firm's ousted workers. His reaction to the Toledo, Ohio, streetcar strike that is the model for the strike in *Sister Carrie* is even more telling. "Without knowing anything of the merits of the case, my sympathies were all with the working man," he would write in *A Book About Myself*. "I had seen enough of strikes, and of poverty, and of the quarrels between the moneylords and the poor, to be all on one side."[23]

These differences in perspective show up at once in the approach Dreiser takes to the crowds of striking workers in *Sister Carrie*. In *A Hazard of New Fortunes*, Howells makes us watch most of the streetcar strike from its periphery, but in *Sister Carrie*, Dreiser takes us to the center of events by following George Hurstwood as he goes to work as a scab motorman. Where Howells worries over the implications of the

22. Howells' failure to help Dreiser with *Sister Carrie* is discussed in W. A. Swanberg, *Dreiser* (New York, 1965), 92; Montgomery, "Labor in the Industrial Era," in Morris (ed.), *The American Worker*, 127–28.
23. Theodore Dreiser, *A Book About Myself* (New York, 1922), 372–73.

crowd's violence, Dreiser, without any philosophizing, shows crowd violence as the workers' only strategy against the power of companies opposing them. The result is that the fear of political bias, so troubling to Howells and his editor-surrogate Basil March, is not an issue a decade later with Dreiser.[24]

The meaning of all this for the way we read *Sister Carrie* is summed up in the downfall of George Hurstwood. His story, we must remember, is the social counterpart to Carrie's. As Carrie rises in life, using romance to her advantage, Hurstwood sinks lower and lower. His passion for Carrie begins his undoing. It turns him into a thief and forces him to flee to New York, where, with neither friends nor status, he goes from being part owner of a tavern to sitting in hotel lobbies day after day. The streetcar strike that Dreiser describes in such detail provides Hurstwood with his final chance at a job, and when being a scab proves more than he can bear, Hurstwood loses all hope. His subsequent suicide (the last scene in the University of Pennsylvania's new, restored edition of *Sister Carrie*) is all he has energy left for, and what it reveals is that in the America in which Carrie and Hurstwood live, those who are poor and try to make it on their own are worse off than they know. They cannot avoid being exploited. They can only hope their exploitation somehow improves their lives.

In *Sister Carrie,* the root causes of the strike that leads to Hurstwood's final undoing lie with the companies. It is not the workers' desire to improve their wages that has made them go out, but the decision of the streetcar companies to cut the workers' daily wage of two dollars by hiring "trippers," temporary drivers paid twenty-five cents to man extra cars during rush hour. Like the Amalgamated Association of Iron and Steel Workers, who found their pay reduced by 22 percent prior to the Homestead Lockout, and the Pullman workers, who experienced wage cuts averaging 25 percent before their strike, Dreiser's streetcar workers have been forced into a situation that leaves them little recourse. Their situation is desperate, and, in making it so, Dreiser provides a framework for his novel's conclusion. Even as he is about to become a scab, Hurstwood realizes the justness of the streetcar workers'

24. See F. O. Mattheissen, *Theodore Dreiser* (New York, 1951), 90–91.

grievances. "Hurstwood at first sympathized with the demands of these men—indeed, it is a question whether he did not always sympathize with them to the end, belie him as his actions might," Dreiser observes.[25]

Hurstwood is just not strong enough to resist taking advantage of the strike. In a short period of time, he has gone from having a ten-room house on the North Side of Chicago to being unable to pay his grocer's bill, and it is impossible for him to worry about the ethics of being a scab. "I can get something. I'm not down yet," the unemployed Hurstwood tells himself as he goes off to Brooklyn to take a motorman's job. This belief is shared by other scabs he meets, "queer, hungry-looking individuals, who looked as if want had driven them to desperate means." Like the scabs Upton Sinclair would describe six years later in the Chicago strike scenes of *The Jungle,* these are men who have fallen below the level of working class. They remain aware, however, of the significance of their actions. Their thoughts are an extension of Hurstwood's reaction to the strike. "I don't blame these fellers for strikin'," says one. "They've got the right of it, all right, but I had to get something to do." Another adds, "You could starve, by Jesus, right in the streets, and there ain't most no one would help you."[26]

For the union men who have held steady jobs with the streetcar companies, the result is a double bind. They have had their wages cut to the bone by their employers, and they are the victims of unemployed men who are actually worse off than they. They cannot, even if they wish, confine their dispute with the streetcar companies to an endurance contest of seeing who can hold out the longest. The companies want total victory, nothing less, as a circular distributed by the Atlantic Avenue Railroad makes clear:

> The motormen and conductors and other employees of this company having abruptly left its service, an opportunity is now given to all loyal men who have struck against their will to be reinstated. . . .

25. The figures are in both cases average. See Foner, *History of the Labor Movement in the United States,* II, 207; Almont Lindsey, *The Pullman Strike* (Chicago, 1942), 96–98. Theodore Dreiser, *Sister Carrie* (New York, 1981), 409.
26. Dreiser, *Sister Carrie,* 411, 414, 415.

Such men will be given employment (with guaranteed protection) in the order in which such applications are received. . . . Otherwise, they will be considered discharged, and every vacancy will be filled by a new man as soon as his services can be secured.[27]

This statement is similar to the Carnegie Steel Company's prelockout declaration: "Hereafter the Homestead steel works will be operated as a non-union mill. . . . There will be, no doubt, a scale of wages; but we shall deal with the men individually, not with any organization." To Hurstwood, what the circular says is reassuring. He stops agonizing over his decision to become a scab, convinced now that the union workers will lose, no matter what he chooses to do. "They can't win," he tells himself. "They haven't any money. The police will protect the companies. They've got to. The public has got to have its cars."[28]

Hurstwood's assessment echoes the conclusion Conrad Dryfoos reaches in *A Hazard of New Fortunes* when he concedes that the workers he cares about will have to give in, even though a strike is the only way for them to get justice. But at this point, Dreiser's narrative again diverges radically from Howells'. Whereas the latter focuses principally on the desperation of his strikers' actions, Dreiser focuses on the desperation plus strength. This difference is immediately noticeable in the local support the strikers get in *Sister Carrie*. In *A Hazard of New Fortunes*, the crowds of striking workers are, despite the presence of other poor in the city, always shown alone or in an antagonistic relationship to the public. By contrast in *Sister Carrie* the crowds of strikers operate from a base of popular support in Brooklyn. In their attacks on the trains run by the scabbing motormen and police, they get help from the surrounding community. A boy with a milk bucket, an old Irish woman, and a little girl, all harass Hurstwood on the trips he makes, and the police guarding Hurstwood's train are forced into a defensive posture. Indeed, in Dreiser's narrative the police themselves are not uniformly antistrike. They do their duty and protect the streetcars, but as Dreiser

27. *Ibid.*, 410.
28. Carnegie Steel declaration quoted in Leon Wolff, *Lockout: The Story of the Homestead Strike of 1892* (New York, 1965), 91; Dreiser, *Sister Carrie*, 410.

notes of the first policeman Hurstwood encounters, "In his heart of hearts, he sympathized with the strikers and hated this 'scab.' . . . Strip him of his uniform, and he would have soon picked his side."[29]

For the strikers, local support is of immense importance, and they add to it their own class-consciousness. Dreiser's novel reflects the fact that the 1890s were the era of the sympathy strike and saw the rise of union leaders such as Eugene Debs, who, in contrast to so many crafts-bound unionists of the past, believed that "the forces of labor must unite" to include all those "left out in the cold to endure the pitiless storms of corporate power."[30] Hurstwood is constantly asked to walk off the job and join the strike, and he is asked in terms that imply those on strike believe he is one of them. "Won't you come out, pardner, and be a man? Remember we're fighting for decent day's wages, that's all. We've got families to support," Hurstwood is told one day. And at other times the appeals to him are even more personal. " 'Listen pardner,' said the leader ignoring the policeman and addressing Hurstwood, 'We're all regular working men, like yourself. If you were a regular motorman, and had been treated as we've been, you wouldn't want anyone to come in and take your place, would you?' "[31]

The failure of such appeals forces the strikers to abandon conventional picketing in favor of violence, and Dreiser carefully notes the shift in their strategy:

> On this the fourth day of the strike, the situation had taken a turn for the worse. The strikers, following the counsel of their leaders and the newspaper, had struggled peaceably enough. There had been no great violence done. . . .
> Idleness, however, and the sight of the company, backed by the police, triumphing, angered the men. They saw that each day more cars were going on, each day more declarations were being made by the company officials that the effective opposition of the strikers was broken. This put desperate thoughts in the minds of the men.

29. Dreiser, *Sister Carrie*, 413.
30. Debs quoted in Lindsey, *The Pullman Strike*, 127. On the role of the sympathy strike in the 1890s, see Montgomery, "Labor in the Industrial Era," in Morris (ed.), *The American Worker*, 127–28.
31. Dreiser, *Sister Carrie*, 426, 423.

But Dreiser will not let the question of violence versus non-violence end here. He goes on to observe that continued non-violence on the workers' part can only defeat their strike. "Peaceful methods meant . . . the companies would soon run all their cars and those who had complained would be forgotten. There was nothing so helpful to the companies as peaceful methods."[32]

With this observation the stage is set for a series of violent clashes between strikers on one side and police and scabs on the other. We are thrust into the kind of labor war that Dreiser reported firsthand for the Toledo *Blade* in 1894 and that the nation as a whole knew that year from Chicago which, during the height of the Pullman Strike rioting, was occupied by fourteen thousand troops, militia, and deputy marshals. Dreiser describes a Brooklyn in which "cars were assailed, men attacked, policemen struggled with, tracks torn up, and shots fired, until at last street fights and mob movements became frequent and the city was infested with militia." At this point, Hurstwood's role as a scab becomes especially critical. As the strike escalates, we follow him to the center of violence and, in F. O. Matthiessen's words, see the response of the crowd "enacted," not merely "conscientiously observed."[33]

The first crowd Hurstwood encounters is typical of the other crowds in *Sister Carrie*. This one is composed exclusively of the poor ("ex-motormen and conductors" and "a sprinkling of friends and sympathizers"), and by comparison to the police, who carry clubs, it is badly armed. But the seeming weaknesses of this crowd do not make it craven or ineffective. It is disciplined and tough, and when the men in it challenge the police, they rely on hit-and-run tactics, moving about like a "small swarm of bees." The following picture of the crowd (described in the first and last sentences in short, direct prose) and the police (described in the middle of the passage in verbose, formal prose) epitomizes what happens throughout the strike.

A swift fist landed on the officer's neck.
Infuriated by this, the latter plunged left and right, laying about

32. *Ibid.*, 420–21.
33. See Jeremy Brecher, *Strike!* (Boston, 1984), 86–95; Dreiser, *Sister Carrie*, 421; Matthiessen, *Theodore Dreiser*, 90.

madly with his club. He was ably assisted by his brother of the
blue, who poured ponderous oaths upon the troubled waters. No
severe damage was done, owing to the agility of the workers in
keeping out of reach. They stood about the sidewalk now and
jeered.

The crowd does not seriously hurt Hurstwood in this scene.
But the names he is called, the stones that hit him, and the
limited protection the police provide him take their toll. By
the time his first morning on the job is over, he is a beaten
man. "The novelty and danger of the situation modified in a
way his disgust and distress at being compelled to be here, but
not enough to prevent him from feeling grim and sour. This
was a dog's life he thought. It was a tough thing to have to
come to." [34]
The afternoon run finishes Hurstwood, and here Dreiser
provides one of the clearest pictures in American literature of
a crowd in full control of its actions. As before, the setting is a
poor neighborhood and the crowd's tactics are those of a guerrilla band, but this time the crowd is much bigger—"a real
mob"—and is sure it can overpower the police.

> The end came with a real mob, which met the car on its return trip
> a mile or two from the barns. It was an exceedingly poor-looking
> neighborhood. He wanted to run fast through it, but again the
> track was blocked. He saw men carrying something out to it when
> he was yet a half-dozen blocks away. . . .
> As before, the crowd began hooting, but now, rather than come
> near, they threw things. One or two windows were smashed and
> Hurstwood dodged a stone.
> Both policemen ran out toward the crowd, but the latter replied
> by running toward the car. A woman—a mere girl in appearance—
> was among these, bearing a rough stick. She was exceedingly
> wrathful and struck at Hurstwood, who dodged. Thereupon, her
> companions, duly encouraged, jumped on the car and pulled Hurst-
> wood over. He had hardly time to speak or shout before he fell.

Hurstwood is both humiliated and seriously hurt, and when
a pistol shot, fired mysteriously from a building, grazes his
shoulder, it is the coup de grâce. He leaves his streetcar in the
middle of the tracks and heads for home—although even

34. Dreiser, *Sister Carrie*, 423–24, 426.

then, not peacefully. "A half block away, a small girl gazed at him. 'You'd better sneak,' she called after him."[35]

The crowds of striking workers in *Sister Carrie* thus prove more than a match for the streetcar companies and the police. Despite the odds against them, they hold their own, and in a city suffering from unemployment, their example is enough to set off a wave of working-class protest. Back in the apartment he shares with Carrie, Hurstwood turns to his newspaper and reads, "Strike Spreading in Brooklyn. . . . Rioting Breaks Out in All Parts of the City."[36] At this point, no one like Basil March comes forward to suggest that there is a middle ground where workers and streetcar owners might meet. Even more telling, Dreiser never implies that Hurstwood could have found a solution to his troubles. A woman as attractive as Carrie may advance her stage career and draw crowds by letting herself be used, but the opposite is true for Hurstwood, who has only his labor to sell.

The alternative to the crowd of striking workers the jobless Hurstwood scabs against is the two crowds of derelicts he joins after Carrie throws him out of their apartment. The first crowd depends on the efforts of "an ex-soldier turned religionist" for its lodging, but their humiliation is total, even when the former soldier is successful in begging on their behalf. The second crowd consists of true Bowery types, and no one, not even the former soldier, bothers helping them.

> These were old men with grizzled beards and sunken eyes, men who were comparatively young but shrunken by diseases, men who were middle-aged. None was fat. There was a face in the thick of the collection which was as white as drained veal. There was another red as brick. . . . There were great ears, swollen noses, thick lips, and above all, red bloodshot eyes. Not a normal healthy face in the whole mass; not a straight figure, not a straightforward, steady glance.

In his 1894 essay "The Men in the Storm," Stephen Crane had described a similar group of Bowery derelicts with great compassion. For Dreiser, who in 1899 made these men the subject

35. *Ibid.*, 427–28, 429.
36. *Ibid.*, 429–30.

of a *Demorest's* magazine article, "Curious Shifts of the Poor," they provide the setting in which to place Hurstwood just before his suicide. Hurstwood's association with such men in the closing pages of *Sister Carrie* demonstrates not only how far he has sunk but also that he is not alone in his fall.[37]

The result is a conclusion in which the political contrast between the hopeless men of the Bowery and the hopeful crowds of striking workers could not be more emphatic, but within the time frame of *Sister Carrie*, it is also a conclusion that goes no further. Dreiser will not extend his story beyond its natural limits to show the streetcar workers winning their strike. His own experience in the Toledo streetcar strike of 1894 militated against such an outcome, as did the national precedents established by the Homestead Lockout and the Pullman Strike, which were both turned into massive union defeats through the intervention of troops and militia. In stopping *Sister Carrie* with Hurstwood's death, Dreiser knew he had done as much as possible within the realistic confines he set for himself to make his political sympathies known.[38]

For Dreiser, who would later describe the 1890s as a period when "the least protest of the mass" was considered "revolutionary," imposing such limits on his novels was not easy. In the quarter century between *Sister Carrie* and *An American Tragedy*, he would not put himself in such a difficult position again. His next generation of heroes, the Frank Cowperwoods and Clyde Griffithses, would stay as far away as possible from any union association. Dreiser would not, however, lose interest in the issues raised by the striking streetcar workers of *Sister Carrie*. Especially in the 1930s and 1940s, he would make his sympathies a matter of public record. Dreiser the celebrity would defend Tom Mooney and the miners of Harlan County, and eventually would join the Communist party. Dreiser the writer would make his opinions known through his political essays. In 1931, in *Tragic America*, he would portray the courts and police as little more than a "corporation tool," and a decade later, in *America is Worth Saving*, he

---

37. *Ibid.*, 465–66, 497–98. See Moers, *Two Dreisers*, 55–69.
38. For a discussion of labor and American culture in the 1890s, see Trachtenberg, *The Incorporation of America*, 232–34.

would extend his argument, contending that the essence of the American working class was its willingness to create spontaneous, often violent "mass movements" when its lawful channels of protest were blocked.[39]

As the Great Depression tightened its grip on America, there would be, however, no shortage of novelists anxious to make the working class part of their fiction. In his conclusion to *Studs Lonigan*, James Farrell would focus on the working-class crowd and the new Popular Front. In *U.S.A.*, John Dos Passos would treat 1919 as a watershed for labor and provide a violent glimpse into virtually every strike lost by unions that year. And in *The Day of the Locust*, Nathanael West would extend the apocalyptic vision of *Caesar's Column* and *The Iron Heel* with his portrait of a proto-fascist mob led by workers who all their lives "had slaved at some kind of dull, heavy labor, behind desks and counters, in the fields and at tedious machines." But in the long run, no writer of the 1930s—not even Nathanael West, whose rampaging mob would become known by even casual readers of American literature—would touch the public as John Steinbeck did. It is to his novels, which Dreiser greatly admired, that we must turn for the next important picture of the working-class crowd in American fiction.[40]

Steinbeck's working-class crowds in *The Grapes of Wrath* and *In Dubious Battle* consist of Okies and migrant farm workers, and his emphasis at first glance seems out of sync with the labor history of the 1930s. The changes that pushed union membership from below three million in 1932 to above eight million in 1939 came through industrial organizing, especially in mass manufacturing. The best-known strikes of this period, from the Fisher Body sit-downs at Flint, Michi-

39. Dreiser, *A Book About Myself*, 408; Theodore Dreiser, *Tragic America* (New York, 1931), 21–22, 203–204; Theodore Dreiser, *America is Worth Saving* (New York, 1941), 238–39.
40. Nathanael West, *Miss Lonelyhearts and The Day of the Locust* (New York, 1962), 177. On West's interest in politics and unions, see Jay Martin, *Nathanael West: The Art of His Life* (New York, 1960), 334–36. Dreiser's admiration of Steinbeck is reflected in his letters. See Robert H. Elias (ed.), *The Letters of Theodore Dreiser* (3 vols.; Philadelphia, 1959), III, 851, 868–69, 877.

gan, to the Memorial Day Massacre at Republic Steel in Chicago, were among nonagricultural workers.[41]

In paying the attention he did to California's farm workers,
Steinbeck was not, however, seizing upon a side issue. Rather,
he was focusing on workers whose neglect epitomized the
worst problems of the depression labor scene. Since the 1860s,
California agriculture had been dominated by corporate rather
than family farms, and by the 1930s, when California was
producing 40 percent of the nation's fruit and vegetables, this
concentration of power had reached a peak. In 1935, one-ninth
of California's farms comprised 80 percent of the acreage in
the state and by virtue of this dominance, the owners of these
farms dictated farm-labor policy. For the 200,000 men who
harvested California's crops, the result was continuous exploitation, and with the coming of the New Deal, they were, as
Irving Bernstein has argued in *Turbulent Years*, forced into
open revolt. There was nothing in Franklin D. Roosevelt's Agricultural Adjustment Act to help them, and the one piece of
New Deal legislation they might have relied on, the Wagner
Act of 1935, specifically excluded farm workers as a result of
lobbying efforts by the American Farm Bureau.[42]

Steinbeck knew these problems firsthand. When we think
of the efforts to document the plight of California's agricultural
workers during the depression, we immediately think of Carey
McWilliams' *Factories in the Fields* or the 1939 hearings of
Robert La Follette's Senate Education and Labor Committee.
But three years before McWilliams published his book and La
Follette brought his committee to the West Coast, Steinbeck
had written about what was happening to California's farm
workers and tried to reach the widest possible audience with
his findings. In a *Nation* article, "Dubious Battle in California," and a series of essays in the San Francisco *News*, later

41. Milton Derber and Edwin Young, *Labor and the New Deal* (Madison,
1957), 3; David Brody, *Workers in Industrial America* (New York, 1980),
82–119.
42. Carey McWilliams, *Factories in the Fields* (Boston, 1939), 48–65;
Carey McWilliams, "California's Migrants," in Daniel Aaron and Robert Bendiner (eds.), *The Strenuous Decade: A Social and Intellectual Record of the
Nineteen-Thirties* (Garden City, 1970), 261–62; Irving Bernstein, *Turbulent
Years: A History of the American Worker, 1933–1941* (Boston, 1970), 150;
Cletis E. Daniel, *Bitter Harvest: A History of the California Farmworkers,
1870–1941* (Berkeley, 1982), 258–60.

published as *Their Blood is Strong,* Steinbeck argued that savagery on the part of the growers was creating a trail of "pain, hunger, and despair" that could only lead the whole mass of labor "to take what they need."[43]

These were not convictions Steinbeck could forget when he began to fictionalize the California labor scene, but he was also determined to make sure his novels reflected the serious doubts he had about the farm workers' struggle. For Steinbeck, these doubts were many, and at the heart of them lay his perception of the crowd as an organizing tool. He saw the crowd as indispensible for the powerless, but at the same time he looked on it as a double-edged sword. He knew, as such short stories as "The Raid" dramatize, that in California farm country, vigilante mobs led by growers were the dominant force. Beyond such specific fears, he also worried about what the crowd qua crowd did to anyone who joined it.

In 1933, long before he started *In Dubious Battle,* Steinbeck expressed these concerns in a letter to his friend George Albee. Once men organize themselves into large groups, he wrote, their humanness tends to change just as the nature of a cell changes when it becomes part of a larger biological unit.

> Now the living cell is very sensitive to outside stimuli or tropisms. A further arrangement of cells and a very complex one may make a unit which we call a man. This has been our final unit. But there have been mysterious things which could not be explained if man is the final unit. He also arranges himself into larger units, which I have called the phalanx. The phalanx has its own memory. . . . And the phalanx has emotions of which the unit man is incapable. Emotions of destruction, of war, of migration, of hatred, of fear.

The mob, Steinbeck went on to say, is simply a phalanx, and "if you try to judge a mob nature by the nature of its men units, you will fail as surely as *if* you tried to understand a man by studying one of his cells."[44]

In the middle of *In Dubious Battle,* this phalanx theory is

43. John Steinbeck, *Their Blood is Strong* (San Francisco, 1938), 29–30. See also Jackson L. Benson, *The True Adventures of John Steinbeck, Writer* (New York, 1984), 295–305.
44. Steinbeck to George Albee, 1933, in Elaine Steinbeck and Robert Wallsten (eds.), *Steinbeck: A Life in Letters* (New York, 1976), 79–80.

posed by Doc Burton, the most reflective figure in the story, to Mac, a Communist party organizer and Steinbeck's principal character. "I want to see, Mac. I want to watch these group men, for they seem to me to be a new individual, not at all like single men," Doc says of the workers who have just come into the strike. Then he adds, "A man in a group isn't himself at all, he's a cell in an organism that isn't like him any more than the cells in your body are like you. . . . People have said, 'mobs are crazy, you can't tell what they'll do.' Why don't people look at mobs not as men, but as mobs? A mob nearly always seems to act reasonably for a mob." Doc disappears (whether murdered or kidnapped, we never know) before he has a chance to answer his own questions. But the issues he raises in this conversation dominate *In Dubious Battle* and make it a novel in which, as André Gide observed, "the main character is the crowd."[45]

What gives the crowd this centrality is what brings Mac and Jim Nolan, the young party organizer he is training, to the apple country of Torgas Valley: a decision by the apple growers, who are under the control of the Torgas Valley Finance Company, to lower by a nickel an hour the wages of the migrant laborers who have come to pick their crops. For the workers, who have spent all their money just getting to the valley, this is devastating news. But it gives Mac and Jim a chance to organize. In an era in which the American Federation of Labor's attitude toward farm labor was such that a spokesman declared, "Only fanatics are willing to live in shacks or tents and get their heads broken in the interests of migratory labor," Mac and Jim are opportunists. Their strategy, like that of the small group of farm organizers the Communist party sent to California during the early 1930s, is to go wherever there is a spontaneous strike or even a rumor of one.[46]

What the workers need, what Mac wants for them, and what they get when they coalesce into a crowd are not the same, however, and it is around these tensions that *In Dubious Battle* lives up to its title. From the start, Mac makes it clear that his concern is not with winning the strike so much

45. John Steinbeck, *In Dubious Battle* (New York, 1963), 131; Justin O'Brien (ed.), *The Journals of André Gide* (2 vols.; New York, 1956), II, 265.
46. McWilliams, *Factories in the Fields*, 212–14.

as using it to further the long-range goals of the party. Before they ever arrive in Torgas Valley, Mac tells Jim, "We got to take the long view. A strike that's settled too quickly won't teach the men how to organize, how to work together. A tough strike is good. We want the men to find out how strong they are when they work together." Mac conceals this view from the workers, and initially he experiences few problems. The men are so dispirited and mistrustful ("If we don't pick 'em, somebody else will," Mac is told when he suggests an apple strike) that any organizing he does seems for the good. When one of the worker's wives has a baby, Mac uses the occasion to draw the men together, and at other times he does what he can to build up London, the man the pickers consider their natural leader. But it is not Mac who starts the strike. It is the collective anger the nickel wage cut has produced and the outrage the men feel when a company ladder breaks under an elderly apple picker. Once the strike begins, however, Mac assumes a very different role. As a crowd, the men acquire a cohesiveness they lacked as individuals, and Mac immediately assigns himself the job of making sure their anger stays on target. "We've got to move while they're hot," he tells Jim. "These guys'll go nuts if we don't take charge."[47] The strain of carrying out this job provides the real test for Mac and in turn raises the question Howells and Dreiser asked earlier: Can an American working-class crowd ever win a strike in which the company it challenges has the government on its side?

In *In Dubious Battle*, the immediate reaction of the growers to the workers' surprising defiance is to try to buy off those they think have organized the strike. Mac's only choice is to stay one step ahead of the game by anticipating what he is sure will be the growers' big move: bringing a trainload of scabs to Torgas Valley. Mac's desire for unity leads him to undermine the informal democracy of the workers by substituting a hierarchical chain of command for it, but as before, the differences between him and the workers seem benign. Mac's long-range interests continue to serve their day-to-day needs. There is no comparing the position the men find themselves in now to their disarray before the strike. Their coming to-

47. Steinbeck, *In Dubious Battle*, 27–28, 45, 90, 91.

gether has brought about instant change in which "in a moment their vague unrest and anger centered and focused."[48]

The gap between what Mac expects of the workers and what they are able to do for themselves does materialize though when as a crowd they go to meet the train bringing in the scabs and the sheriff's deputies the growers have called for. Mac's organizing has not, it turns out, been enough to get the workers over their fears, and they quickly revert back to their earlier behavior. It is as a "straggling parade," not a surging crowd, that they confront the train. Only after one of the party's organizers is killed by a shot fired from a window do the men summon up the courage to confront the scabs and deputies, and at this point their willingness to be confrontational is marred by questions. Can anything other than bloodshed galvanize them? As a crowd, do they know what they are doing? Can they control their anger? Steinbeck never explicitly answers any of these questions, but his description of the crowd's newfound bravery as trancelike reflects his pessimism. "The guards were frightened; riots they could stop, fighting they could stop; but this slow, silent movement of men with the wide eyes of sleep-walkers terrified them," he notes. The scene ends with Mac and the strikers forcing the police and scabs to back down, but we are now a long way from the time when the collective anger of the men was a sign of their overcoming their "vague unrest." Doubts that were not apparent in the early chapters of *In Dubious Battle* begin surfacing with frequency. As the growers try to regain momentum with new violence, the workers respond with increasingly brutal violence of their own. Mac himself starts to lose perspective. He becomes unwilling to acknowledge the toll his organizing is taking. When a local supporter is beaten up by a vigilante mob, Mac's only reply is, "I can't take the time to think about the feelings of one man. . . . I'm too busy with big bunches of men."[49]

At this stage of the strike, *In Dubious Battle* remains nonetheless overwhelmingly prolabor. Steinbeck has so carefully delineated the exploitive situation the apple pickers are in that we continue to give them every benefit of the doubt. Mac

48. *Ibid.*, 89.
49. *Ibid.*, 145, 148, 89, 183.

tells Doc that in a struggle such as this, where one side has all the guns and money, there is no such thing as good taste, and his remark rings with authority. After their train-yard confrontation, it makes sense for the workers to band together in small crowds and drive off the scabs who have come to take their jobs, and it is logical for Mac to use the funeral of the murdered party organizer to build support for the strike. The positive results of his strategy are everywhere to see. The growers' association offers to restore the men's wages to twenty cents an hour, and the men sense their own power. This is the kind of brief triumph the Communist-led Cannery and Agricultural Workers International Union achieved in 1933 following workers' deaths at Pixley and Arvin, California, and Steinbeck captures both the fragility and the importance of the moment. Mac has, at this juncture, earned the right to claim, "It doesn't make any difference if we lose. Here's nearly a thousand men who've learned how to strike."[50]

Mac cannot let well enough alone, however, and what happens after this point so changes the balance of the novel that all that Mac has accomplished and all that follows from the men coming together as a crowd turn suspect. This is not to say that the politics of *In Dubious Battle* become progrower. It is rather that the doubts Steinbeck voiced about the crowd in his 1933 letter to George Albee and that Doc repeats take on new significance. Instead of accepting his gains, Mac, who all along has predicted the growers would start shooting and "get away with it," starts using the crowd more and more exploitively. "What they need is blood," Mac says of a crowd he wants to excite so that it will break down a police barricade set up to prevent picketing, and sure enough it is blood (this time the beating of a provocateur sent by the growers) that sets the men off. As the strike drags on, Mac's reliance on the strength of the crowd becomes inseparable from his admission that the crowd cannot be controlled, and what we are left with is a situation in which Mac acknowledges virtually all of Doc's earlier fears. "People think a mob is wasteful, but I've seen plenty; and I tell you, a mob with something it wants to do is just about as efficient as trained soldiers," Mac says in

50. Daniel, *Bitter Harvest*, 213–17; Steinbeck, *In Dubious Battle*, 258.

one breath, and then in another confesses, "It *is* a big animal. It's different from the men in it. . . . It doesn't want the same things men want—it's like Doc said—and we don't know what it'll do."[51]

By the conclusion of *In Dubious Battle,* we end up with a far more troubled picture of the strike and the crowd than we started with, and it becomes easy to see why Steinbeck would declare, "The book is brutal. I wanted to be merely a recording consciousness, judging nothing, simply putting down the thing. I think it has the thrust, almost crazy, that mobs have." If Mac had stopped his organizing when the violence of the strike was limited and the growers offered to restore the wage cut, we could accept his claim that the strike was "worth it," because it radicalized the men, showing them "how much capital thinks of 'em" and "what they've got to do."[52] By the novel's finish, however, we do not have any evidence that on the whole the men have internalized Mac's teaching. Given Mac's view of the crowd, plus the sacrifices he has asked of the men when sacrifice was futile, it seems likely the only lessons a thoughtful worker will draw from events are cynical ones. As the book closes we see Mac once more using a death (this time that of his protégé Jim Nolan) to rouse the men, but the speech he gives here is so similar to the one he made at the first funeral that what we are struck by is the calculation of his performance. It makes us suspect that, if Mac is persuasive enough, the men who listen to him will again be victimized. Indeed, if the conclusion of *In Dubious Battle* had been Steinbeck's final word on the working-class crowd, there would be every reason to see him as a "dubious" partisan of labor.

As it is, within the context of Steinbeck's 1930s writing what the conclusion of *In Dubious Battle* really speaks to are his suspicions about professional organizers—and more particularly, his second thoughts about the agenda the Communist party brought to the fields in California during its union drives in 1933 and 1934. When we turn from *In Dubious*

---

51. Steinbeck, *In Dubious Battle,* 140, 282, 288.

52. Steinbeck to George Albee, January 15, 1935, in E. Steinbeck and Wallsten (eds.), *Steinbeck: A Life in Letters,* 98; Steinbeck, *In Dubious Battle,* 292, 293.

Battle to *The Grapes of Wrath,* this perspective emerges very distinctly. The organizing process that is portrayed as so manipulative when carried out by Mac and Jim on behalf of the party is treated with great sympathy when it is carried out by Jim Casey and Tom Joad, two initially apolitical figures. There is no doubt about the sincerity of Tom and Casey. Nor is there any question that the authorial voice of *The Grapes of Wrath* is that of the John Steinbeck who, in *Their Blood is Strong,* insisted that "until agricultural labor is organized and until the farm laborer is represented in the centers where his wage is decided, wages will continue to be depressed and living conditions will grow increasingly impossible." [53]

Steinbeck's belief in an organizing based on common sense rather than ideology is reflected in a conversation in *The Grapes of Wrath* where a worker, told that a "red" is anyone who wants thirty cents an hour when the going rate is twenty-five, says that in that case "we're all reds." The conversation is a putdown of a grower who has been red-baiting, but most of all, it tells us that the organizing needed for an American working-class movement farm people will join must be pragmatic and traditional in nature. Steinbeck returned to this idea again and again. It led him to take the title for *The Grapes of Wrath* from "The Battle Hymn of the Republic" and to say of his choice, "I like it because it is a march and this book is a kind of march . . . in our own revolutionary tradition." By the same logic, Steinbeck also saw the Okie migration to California as a political turning point. He was sure the massive entry of "white and American" workers into the California labor scene would make it impossible for growers to use the same terror tactics they had employed against Asians and Mexicans, who had been looked on as "foreign peons." [54]

This belief that California's farm-labor struggles were truly American in character and required organizing similar in outlook is constantly reflected in the interchapters of *The Grapes of Wrath.* There, Steinbeck dwells on the fact that the new migrants to California, in contrast to the "serfs" previously

53. Steinbeck, *Their Blood is Strong,* 29–30.
54. John Steinbeck, *The Grapes of Wrath* (New York, 1974), 407; Steinbeck to Elizabeth Otis, September 10, 1938, in E. Steinbeck and Wallsten (eds.), *Steinbeck: A Life in Letters,* 171; Steinbeck, *Their Blood is Strong,* 28.

imported by the growers, are a displaced "agrarian folk" who believe that their past ("We ain't foreign. Seven generations back Americans") entitles them to a decent life. In a passage that sums up the steps he sees transforming the Okie migration into a political movement, Steinbeck writes:

> One man, one family driven from the land. . . . And in the night one family camps in a ditch and another family pulls in and the tents come out. The two men squat on their hams and the women and children listen. . . . "We lost *our* land." The danger is here, for two men are not as lonely and perplexed as one. And from this first "we" there grows a still more dangerous thing: "I have a little food" plus "I have none." If from this problem the sum is "We have a little food," the thing is on its way, the movement has direction. Only a little multiplication now, and this land, this tractor are ours.

What follows from these interchapters is the kind of perspective that prompted Carey McWilliams in his 1939 testimony before the La Follette committee to insist that *The Grapes of Wrath* contains a "better understanding of the economic and social implications of large-scale corporate farming in California" than does any official publication on the subject.[55] But within the context of *The Grapes of Wrath*, this overview goes one step further. It provides a framework for seeing the transition the Joads, especially Tom, will make from isolation to a politics in which the working-class crowd is a natural outcome.

The transformation begins with Ma Joad. At the start, she is a traditional mother whose life centers on her family. "All we got is the family unbroke," she declares as the Joads begin their western journey. "I ain't scared while we're all here, all that's alive, but I ain't gonna see us bust up." What makes her story so telling is that the longer the Joads travel, the more often Ma's generosity carries her beyond her original sense of family. First Casey and then the Wilsons are treated as "kin," and by the time the Joads reach Bakersfield, Ma does not even have to know the people she befriends. When a group of migrant children gather around the Joads' tent at mealtime, Ma

55. Steinbeck, *The Grapes of Wrath*, 316, 385, 317–18, 206; C. Mc-Williams, "California's Migrants," in Aaron and Bendiner (eds.), *The Strenuous Decade*, 262.

shares the stew she is cooking, even though it means her own family does not get enough. Feeding the children is an instinctive gesture on Ma's part, but she knows what it has committed her to, and by the end of *The Grapes of Wrath*, she has no trouble putting it into words. "Use'ta be the fambly was fust. It ain't so now," Ma declares. "It's anybody. Worse off we get, the more we got to do."[56]

Like Rose of Sharon, who at the close of *The Grapes of Wrath* feeds a starving man with the milk from her breasts, Ma is never able to take her new sense of family beyond personal gesture, but in terms of the changes that come over the Joad family, it is neither realistic nor necessary that she do so. Her example has paved the way for Tom to become an organizer, and as the Joads are about to leave Oklahoma, Ma even anticipates the political course he will follow. In a dream she has, Ma realizes that the anger her family and others like them are feeling could be a tremendous social force if it were acted on collectively. "I got to thinkin' an' dreamin' an' wonderin'. They says there's a hun'erd thousand of us shoved out. If we was all mean the same way, Tommy—they wouldn't hunt nobody down," she tells her son.[57] It is difficult to imagine a clearer political message, and when Tom turns to Casey for guidance, he finds Ma's thoughts restated in organizer's terms.

Unlike Mac, Jim Casey is not, however, an organizer who from the start is sure he has all the answers. At the beginning of *The Grapes of Wrath*, Casey is changing from a fire-and-brimstone preacher to someone who believes in the holiness of man, and his first political act—joining Tom in preventing a deputy from unjustly arresting a man, then accepting full blame for what they both have done—is motivated by pure kindness. When Casey meets up with Tom again in California, he is, however, a different man. His time in jail has, he says, been like Jesus' time in the wilderness, and he now sees his calling as that of an organizer. At the Hooper Ranch, where Tom is working despite a strike, Casey begins to fill him in on what he has learned, telling him that as soon as the strike is broken, the wages Tom is getting will be lowered. This lesson is cut short when Casey is murdered by the kind

56. Steinbeck, *The Grapes of Wrath*, 231, 606.
57. *Ibid.*, 104.

of crowd Steinbeck most despised—a vigilante mob. But the impact of what Casey has told Tom, plus what Tom has seen of the growers' opposition to the mild organizing at the government camps, is enough to change him. Like Casey, he becomes a man committed to helping others.

It is not a conversion that is allowed to bloom over time. In trying to defend Casey from the vigilantes who kill him, Tom in turn kills a man and must himself become a fugitive. But what is significant about his flight—and gives it such purpose—is that it is not the flight of someone concerned primarily with his own survival. Everything Casey has said about how "a fella ain't no good alone" comes back to Tom as he prepares to leave his family, and he takes to the road with the idea of himself becoming an organizer. He remembers the crowd of striking pickets outside the Hooper Ranch and says to his mother, "I been wonderin' if all our folks got together an' yelled like them fellas yelled." Then he goes beyond specific memory and declares, "I'll be ever'where—wherever you look. Wherever they's a fight so hungry people can eat, I'll be there. Wherever they's a cop beatin' up a guy, I'll be there."[58]

In its tone and imagery, this vision makes us think more of the haunted migrants of Dorothea Lange's photographs than of such traditional 1930s unionists as the embattled steelworkers of Philip Evergood's painting *American Tragedy*. But within the context of *The Grapes of Wrath*, Tom's final vision suggests anything but softness. The opposite is the case—Tom's politics are so clear at this point that they take *The Grapes of Wrath* beyond the sentimentality it would have if its closing symbolism were limited (as is so often charged) to Rose of Sharon nursing a dying man. What Tom imagines is not an impossible future but the emergence of a working-class crowd composed of and led by men like himself: the Dust Bowl migrants Steinbeck described in *Their Blood is Strong* as "small farmers who have lost their farms, or farm hands who have lived with the family in the old American way."[59] In Tom's soliloquy we have a condensed version of Steinbeck's political thinking at the end of the 1930s. What Tom says not only takes into account Steinbeck's mid-Depression jour-

58. *Ibid.*, 570, 571, 572.
59. Steinbeck, *Their Blood is Strong*, 3.

nalism, it goes beyond the ambiguities of *In Dubious Battle* to breathe new life into the very crowd a professional organizer such as Mac assumed could only be controlled through manipulation.

For all the attention he lavishes on Tom's vision of the future, Steinbeck will not, however, take the crucial next step and show that vision becoming reality. We are reminded that here, as in the previous half century of American fiction, the working-class crowd is never shown winning a lasting victory. No matter who or what its original target, by virtue of the potential social threat it represents, the working-class crowd is forced to take on the police and the government. Although it may, as in *Sister Carrie*, gain a momentary advantage, that is the best we see it doing. In the fiction of America's social realists, there are too many powerful men who believe, as one of William Dean Howells' characters observes, that, if left alone, the crowd would "override the laws and paralyze the industries of a country."[60]

To a European novelist such as Emile Zola, the way around such a historical impasse was to assume a prophetic voice and predict, as in *Germinal*, the rise of the working-class crowd from its own ashes. But in America neither Howells, nor Dreiser, nor Steinbeck will suggest that the working-class crowd has sufficient depth of support to be a true revolutionary vanguard. They may believe in the kind of working-class republicanism that in the post-Civil War years prompted union leader William Sylvis to describe his iron moulders as "the bone and muscle of the nation, the very pillars of our temple of liberty," but they will not write as if such a belief had the force of history behind it. As a result from 1890 through the New Deal, the working-class crowd of American fiction is left with relatively little room in which to prove its worth. It claims our sympathy, but its power is constantly suspect. While it changes shape and strategy, it does not, like the industries with which it must cope, become increasingly sophisticated generation after generation. Yet, for the poor of American fiction, the absence of a working-class crowd

60. Howells, *A Hazard of New Fortunes*, 395.

would be an unmitigated disaster. They would be lost without it. In the America in which they work, there is no labor party they can vote for, no radical tradition from which they draw strength. The crowd provides them, as nothing else does, with a chance to resist their victimization and to express their consciousness of the position they find themselves in as a class.[61]

61. See Montgomery, "Strikes in Nineteenth-Century America," 99–100.

IV

The Rise of the Media Crowd

With the start of World War II, the economic conditions that made the working-class crowd such a prominent feature of American life in the 1930s disappeared. In the eighteen months between June, 1940, and December, 1941, the number of unemployed people dropped from 8.5 to less than 4 million. With America's official entry into the war, worker scarcity, not job scarcity, became the central problem for the nation. For the unions, the result was that the last barriers to mass-production organizing were suddenly removed. Large-scale union organizing begun under the impact of the Depression was, as David Brody writes in *Workers in Industrial America*, finished during the war, with the Roosevelt administration pursuing policies that deliberately promoted union growth.[1] Between 1941 and 1945, union membership jumped from 10.5 to almost 15 million as the most intransigent opponents of labor yielded to government pressure to get behind the war effort.[2]

The literary consequence of this change was that in less than half a decade the American writer lost interest in making the working-class crowd part of his fiction. In the early 1940s, when the United States Employment Service routinely filled "whites only" requests from defense contractors and the president had to be pressured into signing into law the Fair Employment Practices Committee (FEPC), the benefits wartime prosperity brought to the union movement were not shared by all, however. When we turn to Ralph Ellison's *Invisible Man*, which comes to a climax with a detailed fictionalization of the Harlem Riots of 1943, we find an America the Depression has not left behind and an underclass for whom the crowd re-

1. David Brody, *Workers in Industrial America* (New York, 1981), 112, 136, 144.
2. John Blum, *V Was for Victory* (New York, 1977), 140.

112

mains the most important vehicle of political expression. The Harlem rioters Ellison describes are, if anything, worse off than the migrant laborers of *In Dubious Battle*. Theirs is not the bitterness of being exploited but something far more humiliating: the bitterness of being written off as superfluous and turned into the displaced persons Ellison wrote of in "Harlem is Nowhere."[3] For these men and women, the riot rather than the strike is the form of protest that makes most sense. The grim neighborhoods in which they live, rather than the workplace, are the target of their anger. Ellison will not, however, allow these factors to reduce the Harlemites of his novel to a mindless *Lumpenproletariat*. They are much too knowing for such a judgment, and the political art of *Invisible Man* consists of letting us see the logic and ingenuity behind their fury by filtering events through the eyes of the novel's "invisible" narrator, who both watches and joins the crowds he describes.

To the Invisible Man, the riots he participates in are not simply public events. They are collective moments that sum up his relationship to the society around him, and in a novel that builds cumulatively through variations on the same basic episode, they are important signposts. They mark the Invisible Man's progress from a "homeboy," to a Communist party organizer, to an underground man who, like Ellison himself, has a single, important story he must tell.

In a war-time America in which more than 700,000 blacks left the South for the industrial cities of the North, the Invisible Man's first sense of being caught up in a rioting crowd occurs appropriately in his southern hometown. The episode is not a riot per se but a smoker held by the town's leading white citizens shortly after the Invisible Man's high school graduation. What happens at the smoker is, however, in essence a miniature riot. For the amusement of the whites who have organized the smoker, a group of young blacks are blindfolded and set to fighting each other in a battle royal. What follows is "complete anarchy," then complete humiliation, as the winners and losers of the battle royal, before being paid off in real

3. *Ibid.*, 183, 185–88; Ralph Ellison, "Harlem is Nowhere," in *Shadow and Act* (New York, 1964), 300.

money, are tricked into picking up brass coins from an electrified rug.[4]

It is a painful evening for the Invisible Man, but his life up to this point is such that he ignores the pain. As his black high school's leading graduate, he is rewarded with a briefcase and a scholarship to the all-black state college and permitted to give a Booker T. Washington–like speech on cultivating better relations with whites. It is the scholarship and the speech the Invisible Man chooses to remember, and he leaves the smoker with a feeling of triumph. "I was so moved that I could hardly express my thanks," he recalls. "I felt an importance that I had never dreamed." That night the Invisible Man has a frightening dream in which he opens his briefcase and finds a note in it that says, "Keep This Nigger-Boy Running."[5] But he does not have enough distance to understand the meaning of the dream. Not until he is expelled from college (for not being the right kind of Uncle Tom) and moves North can he begin to come to terms with the contrived violence of the smoker and the contempt with which his speech was actually received.

What gives the Invisible Man the will to reexamine his past is the perspective that comes from being far enough away from the South to see that the patterns of deference he has accepted serve no one except whites. The turning point for him is his accidental involvement in a Harlem eviction riot. The people being evicted are an old couple (the man still has his manumission papers) who remind the Invisible Man of his parents and the South he grew up in. When he sees their furniture piled out on the street, he thinks, "It was as though I myself was being dispossessed of some painful yet precious thing which I could not bear to lose." At first, however, the Invisible Man does not have the nerve to do anything about the eviction. He watches it with shame, as does everyone else in the crowd, and he overhears but does not react to the evicted woman's assertion, "It's all the white folks, not just one. They all against us."[6]

4. Blum, V Was for Victory, 200; Ralph Ellison, Invisible Man (New York, 1952), 19. For a discussion of the parallels between the smoker and the concluding riot in Invisible Man, see Thomas A. Vogler, "Invisible Man: Somebody's Protest Novel," Iowa Review, I (Spring, 1970), 64–82.
    5. Ellison, Invisible Man, 26.
    6. Ibid., 205.

His passivity changes, though, when the old couple decide to go back in their house one final time to pray and are barred from doing so by a marshal. The Invisible Man sees that the crowd is on the verge of attacking the two marshals carrying out the eviction. He realizes that his own feelings, while mixed, are anything but passive toward the mob violence about to take place. "I both wanted it and feared the consequences, was outraged and angered at what I saw and yet surged with fear . . . of what the sight of violence might release in me," he admits. His response to these feelings is to give a speech that is as impassioned as it is ambivalent. Instead of urging the crowd to attack, the Invisible Man reminds them that they are a "law-abiding and a slow-to-anger people" and that for every one of them, there are ten men with pistols ready to carry out evictions.[7]

But the longer the Invisible Man speaks, the more his southern rhetoric is interpreted by the Harlem crowd as deliberate irony. The men and women listening to him hear only what they want to and decide that he is really urging them on. A crowd that had no nerve when it thought it was leaderless suddenly has all the nerve it needs, and before the Invisible Man realizes what is happening, they charge the marshal with the gun.

> There was a rush against me and I fell, hearing a single explosion, backward into a whirl of milling legs, overshoes, the trampled snow cold on my hands. Another shot sounded like a bursting bag. Managing to stand, I saw atop the steps the fist with the gun being forced into the air above the crowd's bobbing heads and the next instant they were dragging his down into the snow; punching him left and right, uttering a low tense swelling sound of desperate effort; a grunt that exploded into a thousand softly spat, hate-sizzling curses. . . . The marshal was spun this way and that, then a swift tattoo of blows started him down the street. I was beside myself with excitement. The crowd surged after him, milling like a huge man trying to turn in a cubbyhole—some of them laughing, some cursing, some intently silent.[8]

The Invisible Man never anticipated this moment for choosing sides, but once it occurs, he does not lose courage. He is

7. *Ibid.*, 208, 211.
8. *Ibid.*, 212–13.

the person the crowd now turns to for leadership, and when he suggests they bring the old couple's furniture back in their apartment and hold a prayer meeting there, his advice is followed. Much to his surprise, nobody questions his directions. "Men, women and children seized articles and dashed inside shouting, laughing," he observes. "It was like a holiday. I didn't want it to stop."[9]

For the Invisible Man, who has been struggling to overcome the white southern standards by which he has defined correct social conduct, it is a moment of tremendous liberation. So too for the crowd, which after its initial burst of violence is calmed by the service it sees itself performing. Indeed, had Ellison chosen to end his story at this point, it would stand as a self-contained tale of a young black going North and shedding the burden of his past. But the eviction riot that marks the Invisible Man's overt break from his past also leaves him with doubts about his future. Where is he to go from here? Another such confrontation would be repetitious, and even this one carries with it a terrible price for everybody else. To the police, the crowd's actions have none of the meaning the Invisible Man finds in them. The police recognize neither the crowd's compassion for the evicted couple nor the care they have shown in returning their furniture. To the police, what is going on is a threat. It is lawlessness, and the scene ends with a squad of mounted troops arriving and the Invisible Man wondering, "What on earth had I said to have brought on all this? How would it end? Someone might be killed. Heads would be pistol-whipped."[10]

For the Invisible Man, these are questions that can be answered only in terms of his new life in Harlem, and they occupy the rest of Ellison's novel. They are not, however, questions the Invisible Man can answer in isolation or that Ellison, who at this time was managing editor of the *Negro Quarterly*, saw as separable from "the reality of Negro life." The Invisible Man's role in the eviction mob has given him instant status in Harlem and has brought him to the attention of the Brotherhood (a fictional name for the Communist party). He must now struggle to find out whether he can be

9. *Ibid.*, 213, 214.
10. *Ibid.*, 217.

true both to himself and to the Brotherhood's version of a "young hero of the people."[11]

The Invisible Man initially denies this tension. His new political life is too exciting for him to admit that it is based on contradictions. The newspapers have publicized his role as a "rabble rouser," and in becoming involved in an eviction, he has identified himself with an issue that, as Mark Naison notes in his *Communists in Harlem during the Depression*, made for particularly fertile ground for party organizing. The Brotherhood, which has had difficulty organizing in Harlem, is only too glad to take advantage of the Invisible Man's sudden notoriety and sponsor him. He is given an office, made its official Harlem spokesman, and sent on a series of speaking engagements that bring him even more attention. The only person who at this time questions the Invisible Man's new role is Ras the Exhorter, a charismatic Marcus Garvey–like figure, who sees the Invisible Man as a dupe of the whites. But although Ras personally impresses the Invisible Man, his criticisms do not. The Invisible Man finds Ras's black nationalism naïve by comparison to the ideology of the Brotherhood.[12]

The Brotherhood itself raises the first doubts the Invisible Man has about the role he is playing as an organizer. After a newspaper story in which the Invisible Man is singled out as the leader of the Harlem anti-eviction movement, the Brotherhood decides he has become too prominent and sends him downtown to work among whites. This disciplinary action bewilders him, but his innocence and loyalty are such that he does not question the Brotherhood's motives. He still sees himself as the man who "rose out of the crowd." Only when he is brought back to Harlem a short while later does the Invisible Man start to think the Brotherhood may be using him in ways he does not understand. "Something was wrong with the whole deal. . . . It was as though I had suddenly awakened from a deep sleep," he tells himself.[13]

What convinces the Invisible Man that his suspicions have

11. See Larry Neal, "Ellison's Zoot Suit," in John Hersey (ed.), *Ralph Ellison: A Collection of Critical Essays* (Englewood Cliffs, N.J., 1974), 59–70; Ellison, *Invisible Man*, 229.

12. Ellison, *Invisible Man*, 251, 271. See Mark Naison, *Communists in Harlem During the Depression* (Urbana, 1983), 19–22, 258–59.

13. Ellison, *Invisible Man*, 229, 319.

substance is the news that Tod Clifton, a young organizer with whom he was very close, has left the Brotherhood. The Invisible Man realizes that Tod could only have concluded that he was selling out the anti-eviction movement when he left Harlem to work downtown. When Tod is later killed in a confrontation with a policeman, the Invisible Man comes to feel even more resentment toward the Brotherhood. At Tod's funeral, the Invisible Man openly challenges the Brotherhood and gives the kind of emotional speech it regards as reactionary. But he is still not ready to go it alone, nor is he capable of making the kind of sophisticated attack on the radical Left that we see in Ellison's essays of the 1940s.[14] Although by now the Invisible Man realizes that the Brotherhood is dominated by whites claiming to know what is best for Harlem, he decides he can be most effective by pretending to obey its orders while putting his own plans into operation.

The Invisible Man does not get to play this double role for long. He is soon swept up in the riot at the end of the novel and, as in the earlier eviction riot, is forced to take a new political position rather than maintain old loyalties. This time, however, choosing sides is much harder for him. The final riot is not, like the riots that have preceded it, a short affair. It lasts for days and forces the Invisible Man to rethink his life.

The shooting of Tod Clifton creates a setting in which "crowds formed at the slightest incidents." But Tod's death is the excuse for rather than the cause of the riot that follows. It is, as Ellison wrote of the 1935 and 1943 Harlem riots, a "free-floating hostility" that brings out the crowds.[15] Most of the rioters the Invisible Man encounters have no knowledge of who Tod was. Their rioting is a spontaneous act, as the Invisible Man discovers upon reaching St. Nicholas Avenue. "Suddenly the block leaped alive. Men who seemed to rise up out of the sidewalks were rushing into the store fronts above me, their voices rising excitedly."[16]

This unplanned activity dominates the Invisible Man's first

14. See in particular Ellison's review of Gunnar Myrdal's *An American Dilemma*, in *Shadow and Act*, 303–317. For a broader discussion of Ellison and the radical Left in America, see Harold Cruse, *The Crisis of the Negro Intellectual* (New York, 1967), 505–12.

15. Ellison, *Invisible Man*, 388; Ellison, "Harlem is Nowhere," 301.

16. Ellison, *Invisible Man*, 405.

experience of the riot, and everywhere he goes, this initial impression is confirmed. The pent-up anger that people have been keeping in check can now be expressed, and they begin helping themselves to clothes and food. It is Christmas without the need to pay for presents, and the Invisible Man sums up the spirit of the moment when he observes, "The crowd was working in and out of the stores like ants around spilled sugar." But soon the looting reaches such proportions that no analogy can describe it accurately. As the Invisible Man encounters new crowds, all he can do is list the goods he sees them carrying.[17]

After a while, however, the Invisible Man's observations begin to sharpen, and he realizes that amid the looting and the destruction, all is not chaos. When he is hurt, people make sure he is all right before they continue on. When a store is black-owned, it is not broken into, and the looting that occurs is done in a spirit of cooperation rather than dog-eat-dog competition. Above all, the riot is not like the Detroit and Los Angeles riots of the 1940s—a race riot. Police and property are attacked, but there is no attempt to take the violence beyond the bounds of Harlem or to seek out white victims. The opposite is in fact the case. In the midst of the rioting, some Harlemites actually take the time to parody the racial violence of southern lynching—they hang seven blonde mannequins from a lamppost.

The key moment for the Invisible Man comes when he runs into a group of men who have carefully planned to burn down an unlivable tenement. Their organization, their concern for getting everyone safely out of the building, and their belief that only such a dramatic act will have an impact on the tenement's owners impress the Invisible Man. He realizes how blind he has been to the virtues of such ordinary people. He says of the group's leader, "He was a type of man nothing in my life had taught me to see, to understand or respect, a man outside the scheme till now." When the building is set on fire, the Invisible Man is "seized with a fierce sense of exhilaration" and cannot stop reminding himself, "They did it themselves . . . planned it, organized it, applied the flame."[18]

17. *Ibid.*, 406, 418–19.
18. *Ibid.*, 413, 414.

This discovery of order and planning in the chaos of the riot is of immense comfort to the Invisible Man, and he throws himself into the crowd, taking pleasure in the "dark mass in motion on a dark night, a black river ripping through the land." His feeling of relief does not last long, however. He is brought back to reality by the knowledge that the "suspension of time" represented by the riot will end and that its immediate aftereffects are going to be negative. The sight of Ras the Exhorter brings this pessimistic conclusion home to him. In the midst of the riot, Ras appears on horseback dressed as an Abyssinian chieftain and begins encouraging everyone to stop looting and join him and his followers in an attack on a nearby armory. This suicidal appeal makes the Invisible Man realize that the reason the Brotherhood withdrew him from Harlem when it did was to enable Ras to grow in influence. Like the whites at the smoker, the Brotherhood wanted a blacks-versus-blacks conflict that would enhance its power. For the Invisible Man, this knowledge comes as a tremendous insight, and he is sure that if he can convey what he has just grasped to Ras and the crowd, he will change all their lives. In what amounts to a public confession, he renounces the Brotherhood and shouts to Ras, "They want the mobs to come uptown with machine guns and rifles. They want the streets to flow with blood; your blood, black blood and white blood, so they can turn your death and sorrow and defeat into propaganda."[19]

But what constitutes an epiphany for the Invisible Man does not constitute one for Ras or the rioting crowd. In this context there is no way for the Invisible Man to share the knowledge he has acquired. All he can do is save himself and predict the counterviolence that the looting and Ras's actions will bring about. "I knew with a shattering dread that the uproar which for the moment marked primarily the crash of men against things—against stores, markets—could swiftly become the crash of men against men with most of the guns and numbers on the other side. I could see it now, see it clearly and in growing magnitude. It was not suicide, but murder."[20]

It is a prediction that is very much on target. The Harlem

19. *Ibid.*, 415, 404, 421.
20. *Ibid.*, 417.

Riots of August, 1943, left six dead (all black) and hundreds injured. However, Ellison does not close *Invisible Man* on this prophetic note. He does not show us what happens when the police arrive in numbers but, like a movie director, cuts to his novel's epilogue, where we find the Invisible Man talking about his past and raising the possibility that he may yet have a "socially responsible role to play."[21] It is a transition that allows us to see the Invisible Man not simply as a disillusioned victim but, like Ellison himself, as a writer obsessed with a complex story. Equally important, this transition allows us to view the Harlem crowd far differently than we would if we were only concerned with the violence it in the end brings upon itself. We are reminded once again that despite the looting and destruction, this crowd cannot be written off as a disorderly mob. It contains a group of men who in their selection of targets (an unlivable tenement) and symbolic gestures (the hanging of the blonde mannequins) raise what since the urban riots and antiwar demonstrations of the 1960s has become the central question regarding crowds: Can the "powerless," by acts of protest that draw media attention, achieve political ends that neither their numbers nor their influence would otherwise bring about?[22]

We do not get a definitive answer to this question from Ellison's Harlem crowd, nor is it necessary that we should in order for *Invisible Man* to mark the point in American literature at which the media-oriented crowds of contemporary America begin to supersede the working-class crowds of the Great Depression. The modernity of Ellison's Harlem crowd stems from a vanguard within it which recognizes that the impression a crowd creates can be more important than any specific action it undertakes.

The irony, as the 1960s have shown, is that such a strategy is ideally suited to a middle-class, college-educated crowd, confident of its brain power rather than its physical might. The antiwar movement of that decade quickly made such a strategy its principal weapon, and in *The Armies of the Night* Norman Mailer gave the public an insider's view of that strategy

21. See Allen Schoener (ed.), *Harlem on My Mind* (New York, 1979), 175–78; Ellison, *Invisible Man*, 439.
22. See Todd Gitlin, *The Whole World is Watching* (Berkeley, 1980).

in action when he described a 1967 antiwar rally at the Pentagon as "that historic moment when a mass of the citizenry—not much more than a mob—marched on a bastion which symbolized the military might of the Republic, marching not to capture it but to wound it symbolically."[23] The irony of Ellison's Harlem crowd employing the kinds of tactics that would eventually be perfected by liberal antiwar demonstrators preoccupied with winning over the press and television is surprising, however, only because the constituencies the two crowds represent are so different. The similarity of the two crowds—particularly each's recognition of its limited power—is in keeping with the way the crowds of American literature have defied stereotyping and challenged us to view American democracy as a collective process epitomized by men in flux, not merely a body of institutions or a state of mind symbolized by an Adamic figure alone in nature.

23. Norman Mailer, *The Armies of the Night* (New York, 1968), 54.

Appendix: The Crowd in American Painting

When we think of the political imagery that our artists have most often used to represent America, what comes to mind at once is its directness and harmony, its difference from the violent political imagery we find in a painting such as Delacroix's *Liberty Guiding the People*.[1] In this regard, it does not matter whether the subject is the Founding Fathers of John Trumbull's *Declaration of Independence,* or the black and white factory workers of Ben Shahn's World War II lithograph, *The Welders.* The picture of America that we expect and have been educated to see is one in which national character is a matter of individual character arising in a setting from which all visible signs of conflict have been erased.

Yet in American art a second tradition also exists, one in which the crowd rather than the individual is the key to political life. When we look at the development of this tradition over the past two centuries, we see that it sheds a far different light on American painting. Not only does it suggest that the political iconography of American art must be seen in more diverse and complex terms than it has been, it suggests that, as far as any number of American artists are concerned, the collective nature of political action is what merits our most serious attention.

What does such collective political action look like? Can a crowd be politically effective and not brutal? Can it represent the nation as a whole without being a tyrannical majority? For American artists concerned with portraying the crowd, such questions are crucial, and—as is the case in American literature—the answers they offer reflect historical awareness

1. For a discussion of the politics of *Liberty Guiding the People,* see T. J. Clark, *The Absolute Bourgeois: Artists and Politics in France, 1848–1851* (Greenwich, Conn., 1973), 9–30.

of the changing role the crowd has played in American life from the time of the American Revolution to the labor wars of the Great Depression.

Nowhere is this relationship between historical circumstance and historical vision more evident than in Paul Revere's *Boston Massacre,* an engraving, complete with political verse, of the Boston Massacre of 1770. Thirty-four years after the Massacre, John Adams would write, "Not the battle of Lexington or Bunker Hill, not the surrender of Burgoyne or Cornwallis were more important than the battle of King Street on the 5th of March, 1770." But in 1770 such a view of the Boston Massacre was by no means a given. Adams' own writing reveals that. He was appalled by the mob conduct of the Boston crowd, not the five deaths that occurred when British troops fired on them. In Adams' eyes the Massacre crowd was a "motley rabble of saucy boys, negroes, Irish teagues and out landish jack tars," and in his courtroom defense of the British troops, he made it clear that there was no way "to apply the word rebel on this occasion."[2]

What changed Adams' judgment of the importance of the Boston Massacre were the political events that came after it. But in 1770 with the Revolution still years away, the reality of the Massacre was not nearly so important as the light in which it was cast, and it is with this situation in mind that we can begin to appreciate the significance of *Boston Massacre.* In an era in which even so accomplished an artist as John Singleton Copley would in his etching *The Deplorable State of America* turn his hand to revolutionary cartooning, art and patriot propaganda were often close, and in Revere's case they were inseparable. Although not an inspired draftsman, Revere was a fine engraver, and time and again, he took other men's work and turned it into patriot propaganda. The results of this "borrowing" are apparent years before *Boston Massacre* in the way Revere changed an English cartoon, *View of the Present*

2. Adams to J. Morse, January 5, 1816, in Charles Francis Adams (ed.), *The Works of John Adams* (10 vols.; Boston, 1850–56), X, 203; *Rex v. Wemms,* in L. Kinvin Wroth and Hiller B. Zobel (eds.), *Legal Papers of John Adams* (3 vols.; Cambridge, Mass., 1965), 266, 252.

Crisis, into *A View of the Year 1765,* an etching celebrating colonial riots against the Stamp Act, and they are apparent in 1774 in *The Able Doctor, or America Swallowing the Bitter Draught,* an engraving in which Revere turned an even more elaborate English cartoon into anti–tea tax propaganda.[3]

When we turn to *Boston Massacre,* we find this same artistic pattern. Revere has once again used another man's work, and once again his engraving is a celebration of collective resistance to British authority. The difference is that this time it is not as easy to be tolerant of Revere's borrowing. In *Boston Massacre* it is not a far-off British artist that he has taken advantage of but Henry Pelham, a Boston painter and engraver, who was hurt by Revere's plagiarism and complained to him, "I find . . . myself in the most ungenerous Manner deprived not only of any proposed Advantage but even of the expense I have been at, as truly as if you had plundered me on the highway." If we are to come to terms with the significance of *Boston Massacre,* it does not make sense to dwell on Revere's plagiarism, however. In this period in which there were numerous American and British versions of the Boston Massacre, Revere's engraving had the greatest impact of all, and what is important to understand is why it was so affecting and what this indicates about the place of the crowd in American art.[4]

The important point to begin with is Revere's political intentions. As a pen-and-ink diagram he did of the scene of the Massacre shows, Revere knew precisely what went on that March 5 night and, by extension, what led up to it.[5] He knew that there had been a long-standing feud between unemployed colonists and British troops, who often supplemented their meager pay by taking extra jobs, and that on this occasion a crowd of colonists, armed with clubs and brickbats, attacked an outnumbered squad of British troops, who panicked and

3. Museum of Fine Arts, Boston, *Paul Revere's Boston, 1735–1818* (Boston, 1975), 114–27.

4. Pelham quoted in Clarence S. Brigham, *Paul Revere's Engravings* (New York, 1969), 52–53. For a discussion of Paul Revere and eighteenth-century rules of artistic plagiarism, see Esther Forbes, *Paul Revere and the World He Lived In* (Boston, 1942), 154–56.

5. Forbes, *Paul Revere,* 130–32, 154.

fired on their tormentors, despite the efforts of their commander, Captain Preston. Yet as far as Revere the political artist was concerned, all of these facts could be put aside. He was after a different kind of truth, and it is only with this revolutionary intention in mind that we can begin to appreciate what it meant for Revere to commit himself to an engraving that showed a sanitized Boston mob, a sadistic Captain Preston, and murderously cool British troops.

The political thrust of Revere's engraving is apparent the moment we look at it. What we are immediately drawn to is not a scene of riotous confusion but a picture neatly divided. On the left, a tightly packed crowd of colonists retreat with their wounded. On the right, beneath a Butcher's Hall sign (a touch Revere added to Pelham's engraving), a line of British troops fire their rifles. This bifurcation of *Boston Massacre* shapes our sense of it, and the closer we look at its contrasting halves, the more we find our initial impressions confirmed. Like the buildings that Revere has carefully rendered, the British troops stand erect and stonelike. They have formed themselves into a perfect firing line, and in response to their captain, who stands behind them with his sword upraised, they fire at once. Not a single British soldier shows fear or hesitation. They could not be more professional, and in the tinted version of *Boston Massacre*, their red coats further emphasize their unity and the bloody toll they take. By contrast, the weaponless crowd shows anything but uniformity or aggressiveness. Although more numerous than the British troops, they are clustered together in a defensive knot and clearly in no position to counterattack. Whatever their sentiments, these patriots have not come to battle, and this is apparent in their response to the murderous fire of the British. Some lie dying on the ground, others carry off the wounded, and one holds out his arm, as if such a gesture might ward off a bullet.

At this point there can be no doubt about where the political sympathies of *Boston Massacre* lie, and when we look at its details, we find they reinforce our initial impressions. The political differences that the bifurcation of *Boston Massacre* supports are extended by the graphic care with which Revere renders the faces of the colonists and British troops. In the case of the latter, their looks are a match for the brutal task they perform. All of them stare straight ahead at their human targets, and all of them look grim. If they are to be distinguished from one another, it cannot be on the basis of any concern that they show. At least two of the troops appear to delight in their task, to be grinning while they shoot. By contrast, the patriots, who in their long coats, vests, and breeches have the air of gentlemen, show a completely different set of emotions. Their faces and gestures reflect fear, shock, and surprise, and when we look at their eyes, we see the variety of responses that characterizes their victimhood. These are men who, despite common beliefs, act independently, and unlike the British troops, who only stare straight ahead, the colonists look every which way. Some stare heavenward, as if hoping for a miracle, others turn to their dying comrades, and still others look to the side, as if the carnage around them were too much to bear.

The result is that, whether we approach *Boston Massacre* with great care or merely allow it to catch our eye, as colonists who first saw it in broadcast form must have done, its political vision remains the same. Yet the matter does not end here. Revere has done more with *Boston Massacre* than achieve good propaganda or add "wings to fancy," to use the words of Josiah Quincy, the attorney who assisted John Adams in defending the British troops.[6] He has rendered for his contemporaries and for later American artists as well a graphic vision of how crowds can be respectable, less violent than those in authority, and, through their collective martyrdom, capable of representing the nation as a whole.

A direct extension of Revere's vision can be seen in Johannes Oertel's 1859 painting, *Pulling Down the Statue of George III,* in which a triumphant American crowd shows discipline (they all work together) and restraint (their target is a statue, not a person) in its revolutionary actions. Between 1800 and 1860 Revere's view of the crowd was not, however, one that American painters automatically adopted. On the contrary, the crucial question posed in this half century by the crowd in American painting is the one Tocqueville never ceased asking:

6. *Ibid.,* 154.

Can American political egalitarianism work when it no longer has a revolutionary cause to advance or Founding Fathers to shape it? In the second decade of the century, this question is raised and then gently dismissed in such sentimental genre painting as John Lewis Krimmel's *View of Centre Square on the 4th of July*. There, against the background of Philadelphia, the peaceful crowds of the new nation are portrayed as the epitome of democratic order and tranquillity. But by 1829, in John Quidor's *The Return of Rip Van Winkle*, we get a very different view of the virtues and representativeness of the crowd. Although Quidor is determined to milk Rip's sleep of twenty years for all the comedy he can, what gives his picture its comic bite is its vision of postrevolutionary America. It is not enough to notice that a portrait of George Washington now hangs where one of George III once did. The nation as a living presence—as the curious village crowd who gape at Rip—seems anything but a vital political force. As Bryan Jay Wolf observes in his recent *Romantic Re-Vision*, the motley townsfolk who surround Rip "bear a striking resemblance to the round-faced, vacant-eyed figures peopling the public spaces in the art of Honoré Daumier." Their expressions are a mix of belligerence, self-importance, and harsh curiosity that do not suggest a brave new republic so much as a "contorted humanity" absorbed by daily life.[7]

Could such a crowd ever work out a compelling democratic identity for itself? It is difficult to imagine how, but Quidor's painting, which is limited by its dependence on Washington Irving's "Rip Van Winkle," does not fully venture into such speculative territory. Rather, it paves the way for our looking ahead to the 1850s, to the work of George Caleb Bingham, whose Election Series paintings hinge on the question of whether the Jacksonian crowd can embody American democracy without muddying it beyond recognition.

For Bingham, the answer to this question is by no means a clear yes. Although he was anxious to do the kind of national picture that would be "illustrative of the history of the west," he constantly voiced skepticism over the West he was living

---

7. Bryan Jay Wolf, *Romantic Re-Vision: Culture and Consciousness in Nineteenth-Century American Painting and Literature* (Chicago, 1982), 154.

in. At his most bitter, following an unsuccessful attempt in 1846 to win a seat in the Missouri House of Representatives, Bingham wrote, "An angel could scarcely pass through what I have experienced without being contaminated. *God help poor human nature.* As soon as I get through with this affair, and its consequences, I intend to strip off my clothes and bury them . . . and keep out of the mire of politics *forever.*" But even in happier times, Bingham had serious doubts about the political process and the electoral crowds he sought to describe. In such historical paintings as *The Emigration of Daniel Boone* and *Washington Crossing the Delaware,* Bingham was willing to memorialize America's coming of age, but he was not prepared to be so uncritical within the context of his own generation. Seven years after his electoral defeat, he would write of his painting *Stump Speaking:* "A new head is constantly popping up and demanding a place in the crowd, and as I am a thorough democrat . . . instead of ̍the elect company which my plan at first embraced, I have an audience that would be no disgrace to the most popular precinct of Buncomb."[8]

When we survey the paintings that make up Bingham's Election Series, we see this same mixture of approval and doubt. From *The Stump Orator* (1847) to *The Verdict of the People (2)* (1855), nothing Bingham paints lends support to the idea that his political paintings are, as John Thomas Flexner has observed, "the most extreme artistic exemplars of America's pre–Civil War self-satisfied optimism." At no point in any of these canvases is Bingham willing to let a single set of feelings dominate his art. On the positive side we see that he has identified national health with a political process in which all (save blacks and women) share and which is embodied in an election-day crowd that cuts across class barriers. But on the negative side we see that Bingham is aware of the price that this sort of Jacksonian democracy extracts. In his political paintings it is not the sobriety of the yeoman farmer or sturdy laborer that prevails but a mix that includes them as well as the town drunkard and courthouse loafer. In the end Bingham

---

8. George Caleb Bingham to James S. Rollins, July 18, 1858, November 2, 1846, December 12, 1853, all in C. B. Rollins (ed.), "Letters of George Caleb Bingham to James S. Rollins," *Missouri Historical Review,* XXXII (1938), 365, 15, 171.

Paul Revere, *Boston Massacre*, 1770. Hand-colored engraving, 9⅝" × 8⅝". Courtesy Museum of Fine Arts, Boston

forces us to confront a country in which, as Tocqueville observed, the people "are not afraid of great talents but have little taste for them."[9]

What these political attitudes amount to in terms of a representative painting and a typical political crowd becomes apparent when we turn to *The Verdict of the People (1)* (1854–55), the work that, as Maurice Bloch wrote in his definitive study of Bingham, "can be considered his major pictorial statement in the handling of the many-figured composition." Bingham was particularly clear about his intentions in *The Verdict*

9. John Thomas Flexner, *That Wilder Image* (Boston, 1960), 146–47; Alexis de Tocqueville, *Democracy in America,* ed. J. P. Mayer (Garden City, 1969), 198.

George Caleb Bingham, *The Verdict of the People (1)*, 1854–55. Oil on canvas, 46″ × 65″. By permission of the Boatmen's National Bank of St. Louis

of the People. "I intend it to be a representation of a scene that takes place at the close of an exciting political contest, just when the final result is proclaimed," he wrote his friend James S. Rollins. "The subject will doubtless strike you as one calculated to furnish that contrast and variety of expression which confers the chief value upon pictures of this class."[10]

When we scrutinize the election-day crowd that overflows *The Verdict of the People,* we see that Bingham has, however, done far more than capture their "contrast and variety" of expression. To their credit, those who make up the crowd of

10. E. Maurice Bloch, *George Caleb Bingham: The Evolution of an Artist* (Berkeley, 1967), 166; Bingham to James S. Rollins, April 16, 1854, in C. B. Rollins (ed), "Letters," 180.

The Verdict of the People show no signs of rancor or class-consciousness. Townsmen of every sort—from drunkards, to men in top hats, to a hat salesman wearing several hats—mingle with each other. The men who by their formal dress seem among the better off do not cluster together or wear more thoughtful expressions, nor is there any way to distinguish those who voted for the winner from those who voted for the loser. Whatever the issues in this election may have been, they were clearly not decided on the basis of class. The irony is that the pervasive cheerfulness of *The Verdict of the People* is also indicative of the painting's political skepticism. The closer we look at the many individual faces in Bingham's crowd, the harder it is to tell if anyone voted for the losing candidate or seriously cared who won. We are left with the impression that for this crowd, what is most important is the act of voting, the political process itself, rather than any specific result it might yield.

The composition of *The Verdict of the People* bears out this mixture of approval and disapproval even more concretely. In the manner of Poussin, Bingham has used the Renaissance technique of arranging his figures in pyramidal masses that give order and balance to his canvas.[11] Yet when we look at Bingham's figure groupings from a political perspective, we see that in contrast to Poussin's, they are often as ironic as they are forthcoming in what they emphasize. *The Verdict of the People* is dominated by a pyramidal mass of figures who appear on the left side of the canvas on the courthouse steps, where a clerk reads the election results. From this group our eye is drawn down a line of heads to the foreground of the painting, where a drunk sits on the ground. Then our attention shifts to the right side of the painting, where a smaller pyramid of figures balances the larger mass on the left and provides a framework for the center of *The Verdict of the People*, which is filled by a shadowy cluster of figures, over which flies an American flag. By all logic, the pyramid of men on the courthouse steps ought to seem more politically engaged than the men on the right side of the canvas, who are

11. For a discussion of Bingham and Renaissance technique, see Bloch, *George Caleb Bingham,* 147–48; Albert Christ-Janer, *George Caleb Bingham: Frontier Painter of Missouri* (New York, 1975), 65–66.

not in so good a position to hear the election announcement. Yet when we try to distinguish these two groups of men on the basis of their political seriousness, we cannot. Many of the men around the courthouse ignore the election announcement (some even play cards), and in the end we are forced back to where we were when we treated *The Verdict of the People* as a series of character studies and concentrated on faces in it. All we can know for sure is that there is a direct visual relationship between the casual manner of the crowd and the casualness with which it treats the election process.

No such ambiguous combination of approval and skepticism is possible though when we move from Bingham's diverse, Jacksonian crowd to the working-class crowds of Robert Koehler's *The Strike* and Philip Evergood's *American Tragedy*. We have already passed the point in American history at which a politician such as James Kent had grounds for complaining, "We are no longer to remain plain and simple republics of farmers. . . . We are fast becoming a great nation, with great commerce, manufactures, population, wealth, luxuries, and with the vices and miseries they engender."[12] By the middle 1880s, too much has happened as a result of America's industrial growth. A world in which personal familiarity could make up for social differences has been left behind. Koehler's strikers do not have the privilege the men and women of Eastman Johnson's *Cranberry Pickers* (ca. 1875–80) do, of working for employers with whom they share a community of interest. Their position is like that of the laborers of Thomas Anshutz's *Ironworkers: Noontime* (1882), who see themselves as a working class rather than part of a larger community that is prepared to ignore economic distinctions.

In the case of Koehler, whose painting *The Strike* was first shown at the National Academy of Design's annual exhibit in 1886, an interest in labor problems was only natural. The son of a German immigrant and machinist, Koehler was by his own admission "very much at home" in the places his father was employed. A year before undertaking *The Strike*, he made his prolabor views known with his painting *The Socialist*, a

12. Douglas T. Miller, *The Birth of Modern America, 1820–1850* (Indianapolis, 1970), 21.

flattering portrait of a radical orator in action, and *The Strike*, in addition to its formal showing, was reproduced in *Harper's Weekly* on May 1, 1886, to coincide with national demonstrations on behalf of the eight-hour workday. For Koehler, who based his painting on the Pittsburgh strike of 1877, completed his work in Munich, and traveled to London and Birmingham to sketch laborers, *The Strike* was the triumph of a lifetime. Fifteen years after its completion, he had no hesitation in observing, "*The Strike* was in my thoughts for years" and is "the strongest and most individual work I have yet done."[13]

What makes *The Strike* so interesting—and at the same time requires that it be paired with Evergood's *American Tragedy*—is, however, that for all its prolabor sympathies, it gives a measured and time-bound picture of the working-class crowd in America. The men Koehler portrays in his monumental (six feet by nine feet) canvas are not prepared for a unified challenge to the factory owner they work for, and it is this historic sense of the American labor movement in the late nineteenth century that dominates *The Strike*.

We see this perspective initially in the balance that Koehler achieves between the factory owner and the crowd of workingmen around him. By weight of numbers, the workers should dominate *The Strike*, and the lone factory owner should be on the verge of being engulfed. Yet this is not the case. There is a visual parity between the two in terms of the painting's dramatic structure, and what this parity points to is that in industrial America, money, not human lives, determines real power. Koehler makes us aware of this by drawing our attention to the spot where the factory owner and his workers stand in confrontation. There we see that neither the owner nor his workers show signs of yielding. In the standoff, the power of one man to affect so many lives emerges. The factory owner appears on the porch of his home, elevated above the heads of the crowd, and everything about him reinforces his position of superiority. His formal clothes and top hat reflect his immunity from physical toil. The brick house behind him emphasizes the solidity of his financial position, and the

13. Patricia Hills, *The Working American* (Washington, D.C., 1979), 9.

stone column he stands against makes him look even taller than he is.

By contrast, the workers of *The Strike*, with their caps and motley dress, have nothing extra or material to define their strength. They appear in the open space between the owner's home in the left foreground and a distant factory in the right background. As our eyes follow them back to the factory we see their strength rests purely on their physical presence. The only way they might be able to win this strike would be by organizing themselves into a cohesive unit, and that is their problem. Cohesiveness is not what we see when we look at these men with an eye to the details of *The Strike*.

The most subtle and revealing social fact of *The Strike* is that Koehler's workers show only limited solidarity. Despite the challenge they have issued, they remain in essence a loosely organized proletariat characterized by varying degrees of commitment. To be sure, some of the men in the crowd are angry and ready to act. There is a worker in a red shirt who confronts the factory owner directly and gestures with his arm, another man who stoops to pick up stones, and in the center of the painting a man with a raised fist who appears to be shouting. But these militant men are not in the majority, nor do we have any indication that they are leaders. When we try to make a judgment about how Koehler's workers are likely to proceed, we can only guess. They do not give unified support to the man in the red shirt who directly challenges the factory owner, nor do they seem ready for violent confrontation as a group. A number of the men question each other rather than prepare for action, and when we focus on the two women in the picture—one stands with her back to the action and scolds her husband; the other stands by the factory owner's house with a baby in her arms and a terrified child next to her—we are left with the impression that these women believe the men have already gone too far.

In the end, it is the poignancy rather than the militancy of *The Strike* that is most affecting. Koehler will not allow his prolabor sympathies to let him give the men he portrays a collective power they do not possess. What we are shown in the final analysis are not hardened unionists but the kind of

Robert Koehler, *The Strike*, 1886. Oil on canvas, 71½" × 108½".
Collection of Lee Baxandall, Courtesy Bread and Roses Cultural Project, Inc., of the
National Union of Hospital and Health Care Employees

"decent-looking" working-class crowd Basil March in William
Dean Howells' *A Hazard of New Fortunes* insists would never
be guilty of "riotous outbreaks."[14] We are still a long way from
the working-class defiance John Sloan depicts in his 1914
Masses drawing, *Class War in Colorado*. Indeed, for the collective militancy latent in *The Strike* to be fully realized
in American art, we must wait for the Depression and the
working-class crowd of Philip Evergood's *American Tragedy*
(1937).

Of *American Tragedy* and his own involvement in the labor
struggles of the 1930s, Evergood wrote, "When I thought of

14. William Dean Howells, *A Hazard of New Fortunes* (New York, 1911),
479.

Philip Evergood, *American Tragedy*, 1937. Oil on canvas, 29½″ × 39½″. Courtesy Mrs. Gerritt Pieter Van de Bovenkamp

my background of Eton and Cambridge and that kind of non-sense . . . I felt very moved to shake it off and to be part of what I was painting. . . . I don't think that anybody who hasn't been really beaten up by the police badly, as I have, could have painted an *American Tragedy*."[15] The results bear out Ever-good's description of his thinking at the time and link his pic-ture not merely to the proworker art of the decade but to such militant 1930s strike paintings as William Gropper's *Youngs-town Strike*, Joseph Hirsch's *Landscape with Tear Gas*, Edward Lanning's *Unlawful Assembly, Union Square*, and Reginald March's *End of the Fourteenth Street Crosstown Line*. In his rendering of the 1937 Memorial Day Massacre in Chicago, in

15. John I. H. Baur, *Philip Evergood* (New York, 1975), 34–35.

which police attacked a march of Republic Steel workers, killing ten and injuring scores, Evergood went far beyond the
social sympathy we see reflected in his *The Pink Dismissal
Slip* (1937) and *Through the Mill* (1940). It is the willingness
of an unarmed working-class crowd (men, women, whites,
blacks, Hispanics) to stand up to a murderous assault by the
police that defines *American Tragedy* and brings to life Evergood's conviction that "there was a need for exposing . . . the
rotten brutality of the company police in the steel strike in
Chicago."[16]

Although Evergood based much of his painting on newspaper photographs of the Memorial Day Massacre, he made
sure that what he painted served his expressionistic ends. As
Patricia Hills has observed, "Evergood is creating an epic picture synthesizing realism of details with images of moral
heroism in order to stir the thoughts and emotions of his audience."[17] Although the workers of *American Tragedy* are
united by their victimization—indeed, they epitomize a 1930s
painter's use of the centuries-old Massacre of the Innocents
tradition in European art—their particular dignity comes
from their struggle to avoid victimization. We see this resistance most clearly in the central figure of *American Tragedy,*
an angry, red-haired worker in a white shirt and tie, who with
one hand shelters his pregnant Hispanic wife (she too is the
picture of defiance) and with the other hand wards off a policeman who comes at them with a revolver and nightstick. The
closer we look at *American Tragedy,* the more we see that
it consists of variations on this central confrontation. The
workers are all neatly dressed (obviously they did not expect a
fight), unarmed (save for a tree branch held by the central figure's wife), and, without exception, caught up in a pitched
battle with the police, who with their nightsticks and guns
are clearly the aggressors. In this fight with the police, who
drive them from the left to the right side of the canvas, the
workers are certain to lose, and Evergood does not sentimen-

---

16. Evergood quoted in Patricia Hills, "Philip Evergood's 'American Tragedy': The Poetics of Ugliness, The Politics of Anger," *Arts Magazine*, LIV
(February, 1980), 138. See also Patricia Hills, *Social Concern and Urban Realism: American Painting of the 1930s* (Boston, 1983).
17. Hills, "Philip Evergood's 'American Tragedy,'" 138.

talize his picture by holding out hope for victory. But in this context a miraculous labor victory is beside the point. What gives *American Tragedy* its political and polemical perspective is the collective militancy of the workers. The very manner of their resistance reveals that they have crossed a political threshold and achieved a solidarity that cannot be erased.

The class-conscious picture of the crowd that Evergood's *American Tragedy* completes thus allows us to see three distinct crowds dominating American art: a revolutionary crowd that in its martyrdom and respectability embodies justification for nationhood; an election-day crowd that by virtue of its egalitarianism suggests the limits and the strengths of Jacksonian democracy; and a working-class crowd that as a consequence of its victimization reflects the need for dramatic social change. The result is a political picture that American wilderness landscapes and portraits of the Founding Fathers have ignored. But more than that, this picture challenges the way we have traditionally been portrayed as a nation. It allows—indeed, it forces—us to see ourselves in terms of images that reflect the explicit political conflict that has been part of our history.

Index

141